20th Century All-rounder

Reminiscences and Reflections of Clive van Ryneveld

Clive van Ryneveld

October 2011

20th Century All-rounder

Reminiscences and Reflections of Clive van Ryneveld

Foreword by John Woodcock

Pretext • Cape Town

20th Century All-rounder

Reminiscences and Reflections of Clive van Ryneveld

ISBN 978-0-9870042-2-2

PRETEXT PUBLISHING
P.O. Box 23199, Claremont 7735 SOUTH AFRICA
www.pretext.co.za • info@pretext.co.za

Foreword

When, in 1902, Cecil Rhodes, the African imperialist with an unstinting admiration for the Oxford ethos, set up a series of Oxford scholarships for colonial, American and German students, exactly the sort of person he must have had in mind was Clive van Ryneveld. Rhodes decreed that those students chosen should "not be merely bookworms." "Their fondness of and success in many outdoor sports such as cricket, football and the like" should count as much as "literary and scholastic attainments" and scarcely less than "their qualities of truth, courage, devotion to duty, sympathy for the protection of the weak, kindliness, unselfishness and fellowship".

As readers of this book will discover, the extent to which Clive has kept faith with Rhodes's wishes is wonderfully to his credit. He has been an all-rounder of the kind and magnitude that is now virtually extinct. University College, where Clive was at Oxford, may number an American President in Bill Clinton among its Rhodes scholars, but none of them, from "Univ" or anywhere else, is likely ever again to achieve more diverse fame than Clive did by playing rugby football for Oxford and England and captaining Oxford and South Africa at cricket, before going on to become a founder member of a meaningful political party and a respected advocate.

When Clive went up to Oxford just after the Second World War, as one of several outstanding South African Rhodes scholars, many of them prominent games players, the university was not only the foremost academic institution in the world, it was also one of the great nurseries of international sportsmen. For better or worse, the second of these distinctions has long since lapsed. Today, to many, the very idea that an undergraduate might ever have written an essay on, say, *The political philosophy of Justice* (Clive read law) in the same week as making a century against Worcestershire in the University Parks or scoring a try for England at Twickenham must stretch credulity.

But between 1947 and 1958 Clive's sporting achievements were indeed the stuff of legend. "Van Ryneveld star of England win" ran the headline over the London *Daily Telegraph's* rugby correspondent's report of England's victory over Scotland in 1949, the manner of which he described as being "the best stimulant" English rugby football had had since the war. In the same year *Wisden*, the cricketers' 'bible', maintained that "the spirited captaincy of van Ryneveld did much to enable Oxford to enjoy one of their best seasons for many years." In the university match of the previous year Clive's seven wickets for 57 runs on the last day had sealed Cambridge's fate.

Back home in 1956-57 he was to lead South Africa's cricketers from the brink of defeat to an honourable draw in the Test series against a strong England side. Having lost the first two Test matches, South Africa won the last two. By the following cricket season, when he captained them against Australia, Clive was already a member of Parliament, though not yet for the Progressive Party, which could be called the conscience of white, English-speaking South Africans and he and 11 others, including the great and indomitable Helen Suzman, launched in 1959.

If Clive owes anything to fortune it is having had the chance to play his sport before it became as specialised and commercialised and professionalised and intemperate as it has. The openings through which, as a brilliant centre-threequarter, he used to steal, are closed off today by huge, fast-moving human roadblocks. Elusive runner though he was, being tall and willowy, he would more likely than not, have been pulverised in the modern game.

In writing about it all, Clive is modest to a fault. Long ago, when they met at Lord's, Sir Pelham Warner would sometimes say to CB Fry, "Come along Charles, let's go and have a good boast." Through having overlapped with Clive at Oxford and cheered him on then, and written about his doings as a cricketer afterwards, I know how much he, too, has to boast about. I also know how scrupulous he was on the field and affable off it. One way and another, he has quite a story to tell.

John Woodcock
Cricket Correspondent of *The Times*, 1954-88, and
Editor of *Wisden Cricketers' Almanack*, 1981-87

Preface

*I*f it had not been for a strong suggestion from Ian (Sir John) Maclure, who features in chapter 19, I would not have contemplated writing these reminiscences. I had put some of my photographs into a scrapbook but had lost momentum to add others. Ian's suggestion came at an opportune time and prompted me to try my hand at it.

What I have written is not an autobiography. It is a selection of reminiscences which were pleasant or interesting for me to remember, and which I thought others might be interested to read. Many other experiences have been omitted because they were better forgotten or to keep the story within limits.

Most of my reflections and reminiscences relate to cricket and cricket people; others to the rugby I played while at Oxford, and to my experiences as an advocate and in parliament. They are written in chronological order and their content is apparent from the chapter headings.

In addition to Ian I would like to thank others who contributed to the book. Stephen Chalke of Fairfield Books gave me valuable comments on my first draft and had it checked for the accuracy of its facts – an important element in a cricket book because of the many cricket statisticians. I am greatly indebted to John Woodcock for his foreword. We were contemporaries at Oxford and he later toured South Africa with Peter May's team as correspondent for *The Times*. My sister Marie Philip and my neighbours Nick Madsen and Professor Tom Bothwell were very helpful with their reactions and suggestions. My wife, Verity, was a constant and valuable sounding board and tolerant author's "widow".

My thanks also go to Pretext Publishing for their efficient production and distribution and to David Gray for his proof-reading of the book.

I wish to acknowledge the use of a number of photographs from various cricket books or journals. As they all appeared over 50 years ago it was difficult to know from whom I could ask permission – apart from three from *The Cricketer* (now *The Wisden Cricketer*), who kindly gave me permission to use them. Three photographs in the chapter on the New Zealand tour to South Africa in 1953/4 were from RT Brittenden's book *Silver Fern on the Veld*. Four were from Brian Bassano: *South Africa in International Cricket 1888-1970*. The photograph which appears on the back cover was a *Sunday Times* photograph which they sent to me. I am confident they do not mind my using it.

Bergvliet, Cape Town
July 2011

Contents

Foreword . . . . / v
Preface . . . . / vii

1. The Early Years . . . . / 11
2. University College, Oxford . . . . / 17
3. Rugby for Oxford – 1947/8 . . . . / 24
4. First Oxford Cricket Season . . . . / 30
5. More rugby, for Oxford and England . . . . / 37
6. Cricket Captain – 1949 . . . . / 53
7. Other Oxford memories . . . . / 60
8. Amateurs and Professionals . . . . / 68
9. Mid-Century Writers and Broadcasters . . . . / 73
10. Western Province Cricket Club and Newlands . . . . . / 84
11. With Nourse's team to England – 1951 . . . . / 96
12. New Zealand tour to South Africa – 1953/4 . . . . . . / 111
13. Currie Cup – 1955/6 . . . . / 117
14. Peter May's MCC team in South Africa – 1956/7 . . . . / 121
15. Australians in South Africa – 1957/8 . . . . / 133
16. In Parliament . . . . / 138
17. Back to the Bar, and the Paarl Riot . . . . / 148
18. A More Rewarding Brief . . . . / 152
19. John Passmore and the John Passmore Trust . . . . . / 156
20. South Africa's Cricket Isolation . . . . / 168
21. Two Rhodes Scholar Reunions . . . . / 172
22. Helen Suzman's Memorial . . . . / 178
23. Cricket after 50 years . . . . / 184

Scrapbook items . . . . / 188
Index . . . . / 193

1

The Early Years

I am a seventh generation van Ryneveld in South Africa, my ancestor Daniel having come to South Africa from Holland in 1759. He became a landdros (magistrate) in Swellendam and then in Stellenbosch. His son Willem Stephanus had a distinguished career as the chief administrative officer at the Cape at the turn of that century. In 1795, just before the first British occupation, he was appointed fiscal (chief financial officer) and when the British occupied the Cape later that year he became the new government's foremost adviser on almost all aspects of the country's administration.

When the Batavian administration resumed control from 1803-1806 he lost his post of fiscal because of his pro-British sentiments but in 1806, the day after the re-occupation of the Cape by the British, he was reappointed fiscal and in 1809 became the Chief Justice (or President of the High Court). His home was Groote Schuur, which was later to be enlarged by Herbert Baker for Cecil Rhodes and was bequeathed by Rhodes to the Nation for use by the Prime Minister.

Willem Stephanus had 10 children. Sadly he committed suicide at the age of 47. One of his grandsons became the Mayor of Graaff Reinet. Early in the 1900's the latter's son Anthony and his grandson Clive, my father, moved to Cape Town and they practised as attorneys in the firm Dempers and van Ryneveld.

I had the benefit of sporting genes on both sides of my family. My father played rugby for South Africa in 1910 when he was 19 and studying law at the South African College, the predecessor of the University of Cape Town. He was one half of a halfback pair, the other half being his lifelong friend Freddie Luyt. My father told me they alternated between scrumhalf and flyhalf, depending mainly on who was closest to the breakdown. He said they had successful blindside movements by having the flyhalf move up to the scrum at the last minute while the scrumhalf moved out nearly horizontally to the blindside. Freddie Luyt's brother, Richard Luyt senior, was at centre with them and the three of them played for SA College, Western Province and South Africa together. Unfortunately my father injured his knee badly in his early twenties and didn't play again but he kept two season tickets on the stand at Newlands until he died.

On my mother's side my uncle Jimmy Blanckenberg played cricket for South Africa in 18 tests from 1913 to 1924. He was a quicker than average offspin bowler who was very effective on matting. In the series against England in South Africa in 1922/3 he took 25 wickets. After the South African tour to England in 1924 he took up an appointment as professional with the Lancashire League club Nelson and he played there from 1925 to 1928, his successor being Learie Constantine. Jimmy married for a second time in England but the marriage came to an end and sadly he then disappeared and in spite of many inquiries none of us have been able to find out what happened to him. The last information we have is that he went to Germany after the war ended in 1945 with the Control Commission. His divorced wife remained a close friend of my mother into their nineties and came out to visit her in Cape Town more than once.

As the Blanckenbergs came to South Africa from Germany and two of my van Ryneveld forbears married Berrange wives I am of Dutch, German and French origin but grew up in an English-speaking home! My wife Verity brought English blood into our family. Her parents came to South Africa from England in 1927 soon after they were married and she was born here.

I was born in Cape Town in 1928, a contemporary of Basil D'Oliveira. A biography of Basil quite correctly noted that while he had to learn his cricket on the uneven streets of Signal Hill, I had the benefit of the best facilities for cricket only a few miles away at the Diocesan College (Bishops). Bishops had a strong sporting tradition. It was the first place in South Africa where rugby was played, introduced by the school's third principal, Canon Ogilvie, in 1861, and cricket had been played at the school from its founding in 1849.

When I went to the Bishops preparatory school in 1936 shortly before my eighth birthday the master in charge of cricket was Pieter van der Bijl, who made 125 and 97 in the timeless test against Wally Hammond's MCC team at Durban in 1938, receiving many bruises from the bowling of Ken Farnes. One could not have had a better mentor. When war broke out Pieter volunteered and saw action in Abyssinia, Egypt and Italy, commanding the "Dukes", the Duke of Edinburgh's Own Rifles. He was injured in Italy. Soon after his return to Bishops he was appointed senior master and ran an outstanding prep school.

The Western Province Cricket Club at Newlands was little more than a mile away. Among others in the same side at the prep school was John Wiley, whose father was the Chairman of the club, and after my father made me a junior member at the age of ten I spent a lot of time there with John and other friends equally keen on cricket. John's father arranged for the club coach, Jack Newman, from Hampshire, to coach juniors in early afternoon nets during the Christmas holidays and we made full use of the opportunity. Jack was a very good coach and he took a great deal of trouble with us. He was one of the earlier coaches to come to South Africa in the county off-season and he settled here. Others who followed and also settled in Cape Town included Tom Reddick, Martin Young, Robin Jackman and Bob Woolmer, and they all contributed handsomely to South African cricket.

Cricket at Bishops and its nearby government school, Rondebosch, was at the time much stronger than at other schools in Cape Town. Our first teams played in the second division of men's cricket. In 1945, when the Western Province schools team was chosen to play in the Nuffield tournament, the interprovincial schools tournament for which Lord Nuffield had provided the funding, seven of our squad of thirteen came from Bishops. A year or two later Lord Nuffield was a guest at a match in Durban in which I was playing and I was introduced to him.

On the Saturday at the end of the Nuffield tournament a South African schools team was chosen which played against the host province.

In 1945 the tournament was in Johannesburg and we played a strong Transvaal team, captained by Alan Melville, at the old Wanderers ground, soon to be expropriated for Johannesburg station. I captained the schools team.

While Rondebosch and Bishops were stronger than other Cape Town schools at cricket, we had stiff opposition when it came to rugby, particularly from schools at Paarl, Stellenbosch and Somerset West, which were Afrikaans-speaking. Rugby was at that time generally regarded as the national sport, not only among Afrikaners. The two special fixtures in the Bishops season were those against Rondebosch and St Andrews, Grahamstown. The match against St Andrews was played, home and away, in alternate years. I missed out on the tour to Grahamstown because the tours were suspended during the war.

Apart from playing a full programme of rugby matches on the Saturday mornings of the two winter terms we had the benefit of being able to watch two good club matches at the Newlands ground every Saturday afternoon. Newlands was the headquarters of rugby in the Western Province and most of the matches in the senior league were played there. But no international matches and few, if any, interprovincial matches were played during the war.

Annually in the Easter holiday the Western Province Tennis Association ran a tournament for junior tennis players in the different age groups. I did not have many shots but could run fast to retrieve and return my opponent's shots. In this way I frustrated better players and became the under 19 singles champion, and with my friend from the age of two, Robert Boyes, also the doubles champion.

In November 1946, near the end of a post-matric year at Bishops, I was chosen to play for the Western Province cricket team in its opening game of the season against Rhodesia. Rhodesia was then an ordinary member of the South Africa Cricket Association, playing in the interprovincial competition for the Currie Cup as though it was a province of the Union. The competition was named after the presenter of the cup, Sir Donald Currie, who was head of the Union Castle Shipping Line, which had the contract to carry the mail between England and South Africa. Rhodesia batted first, led us on the first innings and set us a target of about 300 runs to win in the final innings. I went in to bat at no 6 when we were four wickets down for a little over 100. I was missed behind the wicket in my first over but Ginger Keen and I then had a century partnership and I was not out 90 when we reached our target.

I had little success for Western Province in the other matches of the season but it was a big experience playing interprovincial cricket and coming up against the leading South African cricketers: Alan Melville, who was to captain the touring team to England at the end of the season; Bruce Mitchell; Dudley Nourse; Tony Harris, who played both cricket and rugby for South Africa; Eric and Athol Rowan; and Tufty Mann. Jack Cheetham was captain of the Western Province side. Of our side only Jack Plimsoll and Dougie Ovenstone made the touring team to England. I thought Martin Hanley was unlucky not to be selected, because he was an outstanding offspinner, turning the ball more than any other offspinner I played against. I fielded in his leg trap, and particularly at Newlands, where he bowled into the south easter, you could hear his ball spinning as it came down the wicket. Although Athol Rowan was South Africa's leading offspinner, and a better batsman and fielder, Hanley could with advantage have been taken to England as well.

We went by train to play our away matches, the first of them against Natal at Kingsmead. Dudley Nourse made runs against us, but not without surviving a very confident appeal for leg-before-wicket. We wondered how easy it was to get an lbw decision against Dudley from a Natal umpire. But Natal had a stronger team than ours. From Durban we went on to Kimberley to play against Griqualand-West, at that time playing in the top provincial division. On the journey to Kimberley we heard that there had been heavy rain and when we arrived at the ground on the first morning the wicket was waterlogged, with little prospect, it seemed, of any cricket being played that day. However the groundsman assured us he would have it ready after lunch and to our surprise when we came back to the ground after lunch the wicket was dry. This he had achieved by sprinkling petrol on the wicket and setting it alight, not unknown for a gravel wicket which would be covered by a mat, but unwise for a turf pitch. Not surprisingly the wicket deteriorated a good deal more quickly than usual. We had the advantage of batting first and made around 150. The three innings which followed each totalled less than the preceding one, giving us a comfortable win.

Back in Cape Town we played the traditional New Year match against Transvaal before a big crowd. Today, with so much international cricket and the advent of limited overs cricket, a three or four day game between two provinces (now two "franchises") attracts so few spectators that it does not warrant the taking of a gate; but in 1946/7, soon after the war, with many visitors in Cape Town for their Christmas holiday, and the added interest of the team about to be chosen to tour England, Newlands was full. An incident has stuck in my memory. Western Province led on the first innings and when Transvaal came to bat a second time Jack Plimsoll opened the bowling with a strong south-easter behind him and the wicket-keeper and slips standing far back from the stumps. Eric Rowan took guard in his usual confident (cocky) manner but sparred at Plimsoll's very first delivery, got an obvious touch, and the whole crowd went up in the appeal. Transvaal 0 for 1 and Eric out!

Apart from its good sporting facilities and the good education it provided, Bishops was one of the four schools chosen by Cecil Rhodes to elect a Rhodes Scholar annually to go to Oxford University – a magnificent opportunity for the student fortunate enough to be chosen. I got that opportunity and, after an enjoyable half year at the University of Cape Town, with no end-of-year examination to worry about, I went up to Oxford in October 1947.

2

University College, Oxford

Aged 19 I sailed out of Cape Town docks on a Union Castle mailship in September 1947 for three years at Oxford University. There were a number of students on board going to Oxford or Cambridge and we had a good send-off from friends. The departure of the mailship to England on a Friday afternoon was an event of note in Cape Town's week.

My brother Tony had gone up to Oxford the previous year, also on a Rhodes Scholarship, and he came to Southampton to meet me. He had booked for us to stay in London for the weekend, at a hotel near Gloucester Road tube station, and on the first evening we went to see *Bless the Bride*, one of the musicals which were popular during that era. The most popular at that time were *Oklahoma* and *Annie Get Your Gun*.

Two days later we went up by train to Oxford, my brother to his college, Trinity, and I to mine, University College, referred to as Univ. I had applied to go to Trinity but someone had thought it better for a younger brother to make his own way. It was probably the Warden of Rhodes House, CK (later Sir Carleton) Allen, whose responsibility it was to negotiate with the colleges for places for the newly elected Rhodes scholars. Univ proved an excellent choice, a very good all-round college, keenly supportive of its rugby team and tolerant of students whose sporting activities were time-consuming. One's tutor had to be particularly tolerant in the summer term if one was playing for the university XI because in most weeks we played two 3-day games starting at 11,30am, playing havoc with one's lecture programme.

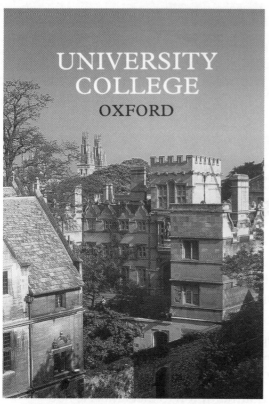

UNIVERSITY
COLLEGE
OXFORD

The Radcliffe Quad at University College, photographed from the Goodhart Building in Logic Lane.

Though disputed by Merton and Balliol, Univ had a strong claim to be the oldest of the Oxford colleges, having been founded in 1249 by a bequest from William of Durham. The college celebrated its 700th anniversary while I was up. Sadly I missed the commemoration ball to celebrate it, as I was on tour with the Oxford cricket team. Univ's main buildings, the main quadrangle and the adjoining Radcliffe quad, fronted on High Street, half way down the High from the centre of the town to Magdalen Bridge. The main quad was built during the 17th century and the Radcliffe quad in the same style in the early 18th. On the opposite side of the main quad from the porter's lodge were the dining hall on the right, the chapel on the left and between them the entrance to kitchen staircase, on which I had my rooms in my first year: a small bedroom and a separate sitting/working room. There was no bathroom on kitchen staircase. I had to cross half the main quad and half the Radcliffe quad to get to one, a cold journey on winter mornings.

I read law with a view to going to the bar in South Africa. It was not an ideal course for the purpose, since the law was English law. However, many principles were the same as in South African law and one could take Roman Dutch Law, the basis of South African law, as one of one's eight or nine subjects. A number of South Africans who studied law at Oxford or Cambridge at that time had successful careers at the bar in South Africa, among them Mick Corbett, who became Chief Justice. He was at Cambridge. Another was my good friend David Knight, at Magdalen. At Univ soon after me was Hannes Fagan, who became a judge of the Cape Provincial Division and in retirement did valuable work monitoring conditions in South African prisons. Two other South Africans who studied at Oxford not long after me, Johan van Zyl Steyn at Univ and Leonard Hoffmann at Queen's, started their careers at the Cape Bar but went on to practise in England and rose to the highest judicial office as Lords of Appeal in Ordinary. Both became Honorary Fellows of Univ.

The head of Univ was called the Master, in my time Rev. John Wild. He had taken over as Master during the war from Sir William Beveridge, author of the Beveridge Report, on which England's welfare state was based. The recommendations contained in the Report were introduced legislatively while I was at Oxford by the Labour government of Clement Attlee, another product of Univ. Surprisingly, although Sir William Beveridge became a member of the British parliament after retiring as Master of Univ in 1944, he did so as a member of the Liberal Party, not the Labour Party.

Since the time of John Wild Univ has had a number of distinguished Masters: Arthur Goodhart, a greatly respected jurist and a generous Univ benefactor; Sir John Maud, British High Commissioner in South Africa before it left the Commonwealth, becoming British Ambassador after it did so; Arnold Goodman, regarded as the leading London solicitor of his generation who was a close adviser to Harold Wilson and later to Edward Heath and was sent in secret to negotiate with Ian Smith in Rhodesia; and recently Robin Butler (Lord Butler of Brockwell), who as secretary to the British cabinet for ten years had been the senior civil servant, and in 2004 while Master of Univ chaired the *Review of Intelligence on Weapons of Mass Destruction*. He was also, and still is, a trustee of the Rhodes Trust.

Univ was one of about 25 Oxford colleges and like the others had a great deal of independence from the central university authority. During my time there I had only a vague idea of how the college was governed. I have learnt more from the reminiscences I have since read in the annual University College Record than I knew at the time. The governing body, as it was called, was composed almost entirely of members of the academic staff – about twenty of them – and the administrative duties or bursarships were undertaken by them, though they had no specialist training. It was only many years later that a full-time Bursar was appointed. Apart from the Master, the senior administrative person in Univ was the Dean and Senior Tutor, Giles Alington, a fabled dean of Univ until his premature death. He was a historian but it was from him that one received one's account for fees and other charges (in my case only for such extra charges as were not paid by the Warden of Rhodes House). Giles was also on university committees and a member of Oxford City Council and Peter Bayley, for whom a Fellowship in English was created in 1949, was appointed junior dean to assist him with Univ duties. My law tutor, Norman Marsh, was the Estates Bursar, looking after the rents which came from landed assets belonging to the College.

In my time there were a little over 300 students at Univ (all men then) of whom about 250 were studying for undergraduate degrees and 50 for postgraduate degrees. Of the 300 just less than half were able to reside in the college; the rest lived in digs. I was lucky to live in college for two of my three years. Our rooms were cleaned by scouts (all male) who also served the meals in hall. The scouts were a special breed, serving the college loyally. One of them in my time, Bob Morris, served in different capacities for fifty years, becoming head scout, and in 1999, in Univ's 750th anniversary year, received an MBE for Services to Higher Education. He started as buttery boy, replacing his brother, who had been called up for national service. One of his early jobs was to go round knocking on the bottom of each staircase with a big mallet to let students know it was time for breakfast. He became a scout and was in time given two staircases and the Junior Common Room to look after. This meant very long hours, with only a two-hour break in the day. Writing some reminiscences in 1990 he said "If you were a servant to the College you put your life in the College. My wife got very annoyed because she said to me: 'I don't know why you don't take your bed down there'".

A specially prominent person in college life was the head porter, located in the lodge at the college's entrance. One collected one's post there and notices were put up on a noticeboard outside it. One also went past the lodge for lectures or other outside activities. So the porter was well placed to know what was going on. The head porter when I came to Univ was Fred (Fred Bickerton). He retired in early 1950 having had 51 years service in the college, most of them in the lodge. His infallible memory for names and faces had made him an institution. He was succeeded as head porter by Douglas Millin, who also became an institution. Like Fred, Douglas had a very good memory for names and faces. He was shrewd and had a lively comment for most situations, expressed in uncompromising language. He was a favourite of Bill Clinton during his time at Univ in the 1960's and when the latter made a formal visit to the college while President of the United States in 1994 he specially requested in advance to meet Douglas and the two had coffee and a private chat in Helen's Court, where the President had had his room.

Of the dons, one's tutor was the person with whom one had by far the most contact, a weekly tutorial at which one had to read an essay assigned the previous week. One had these tutorials either on one's own or sometimes together with a second student, and in the course of a term covered the main topics of a subject. This tutorial system was and is the special feature of Oxford and Cambridge. One also attended lectures in each subject organised on a university basis, but attendance at these was not compulsory. One of my lecturers, in Roman Law, was Tony Honore, educated at Bishops and recognised as one of the school's brightest scholars. After being wounded in the war he went to Oxford as a Rhodes Scholar in 1946, obtained firsts in his BA and BCL degrees and stayed on at Oxford to lecture and become a Fellow of Queen's College and later New College, where he had been as a student. In due course he was appointed Regius Professor of Civil Law and a Fellow of All Souls. In 1988 and 1990 he was awarded Honorary Doctorates at Stellenbosch and Cape Town Universities.

In 1947 when I came to England the country was still recovering from the war and food and many other necessities were still rationed, including clothing and electricity. As I was living in college my food coupons were handled by the college. The meals were limited in quantity and not exciting in quality but perfectly adequate for health, even for rugby. The owner of a well-known pub just outside Oxford who was a keen supporter of the Oxford rugby team thought the team would benefit from a good helping of beef a couple of days before the Varsity match against Cambridge and we were treated to an exceptional meal of roast beef and Yorkshire pudding before each of the three Varsity matches in which I played. Apart from that, one's meat ration was small. In my first year one's egg ration was two per term. Describing life at the college many years afterwards the wife of Univ's Master, Margaret Wild, recalled that the ex-servicemen who came up after the war couldn't believe how limited civilian rations were and on one occasion sent a deputation to the Master in indignation, saying that the Fellows must be eating some of their rations at the high table. The Master got the chef to lay out on a tray one week's rations for one person and to put it in the Hall for everyone to see. She wrote: "There was astonishment and horror when the warriors saw how small civilians' rations were. These rations were actually reduced in 1947, when for the first time bread, flour and even potatoes were rationed." Rationing went on for some years, being relaxed gradually and ending only in 1953.

I knew nothing of rationing when I first arrived at University College a day or two before the official opening of the academic year. Going down to the dining hall for my first meals there were other students who had come up early and we sat diffidently on the benches alongside each other, with little conversation. On the table in front of us I saw a dish or two of butter which I assumed to be for common use and I helped myself. I must have done this for at least a couple of meals before I realised that the butter I was taking was from the individual rations of my fellow students, whose politeness inhibited them from enlightening me.

One could get a very basic meal at a subsidised "British Restaurant" at nominal cost, something like a shilling, and from time to time when we felt the need we cycled there to fill up.

I was lucky to miss the very cold winter of 1946/7, which saw Britain's most severe and protracted spell of bad weather of the 20th century. With coal strictly rationed and electricity cut off for five hours a day across the nation's households, it would have been difficult to keep warm. Electricity was still rationed during the two years I was in residence. The pre-war luxury of a fire in one's room was no longer on offer; instead one had a small electric heater with two bars and one could have one bar on for something like two hours or two bars for one hour. Fortunately after the cold winter of 1946/7 the following two winters were mild.

Rugby and cricket played a very big part in my three years at Oxford but as I was playing for the university I had limited opportunities to play for Univ in inter-college matches. The exception was the inter-college rugby competition in the Hilary term, which ran from January to March, after the all-important annual "Varsity match" against Cambridge in December. It was a knock-out competition known as "cuppers". Univ won the competition in my first year. Twenty-three colleges entered teams. Univ had two blues in Alan Stewart, a New Zealand Rhodes Scholar, and myself and two blues-to-be in Trevor Wilson, a flank, and Nick Gent, a second-row forward, as the lock position was called in England. We beat Pembroke, Queen's and Magdalen by comfortable margins in the first three rounds and came up against Brasenose (BNC) in the semi-final. Univ and BNC had the strongest rugby reputations at that time and we narrowly survived the contest by 9-7. In the final we beat Balliol convincingly 19-0. This was followed by a "bump supper" celebration in the college, during which beer flowed freely.

3

Rugby for Oxford – 1947/8

The start of the academic year in October was also the beginning of the rugby season. My brother Tony had played in the strong Oxford team of the previous year, captained by Ossie Newton Thompson, which had defeated Cambridge 15-5 at Twickenham. Probably because of this I was invited to play an early match for the Greyhounds against the Oxford team. The Greyhounds could be described loosely as Oxford's second team, but were something more than that. Probably forty to fifty players could play for the Greyhounds during a season, since they played against a variety of teams, including one or two school teams, such

Caption in the *Isis*: "Playing for Oxford today, the Ryneveld brothers Clive and Anthony". Tony played flank (wing forward). I was at centre.

as nearby Radley, and sides were chosen with the strength of the opposition in mind. During my time at Oxford Greyhound teams twice went on tour to France at Easter, on the first occasion playing matches in Italy as well as France, and these teams included a number of blues. The early season match against the provisional Oxford XV was in the nature of a trial for the university side. It ended in a win for the provisional XV by 21 points to 16 as a result of a late goal. I scored a try and kicked two conversions and a penalty. Before long I got my chance in the Oxford team.

From then to the end of November, when the Varsity match was played at Twickenham, the Oxford team played at least one game a week, sometimes two, against leading clubs. We beat Leicester 16-10 at Leicester and lost to Richmond 8-13 at Oxford. We beat Blackheath 12-3 away and Harlequins 24-0 at Twickenham, their home ground.

There were two special matches, against Major Stanley's XV and against the international Australian team touring the United Kingdom. Major Stanley had been the OURFC representative on the committee of the Rugby Football Union (the official name of the English Rugby Football Union) and had also been an England selector. From soon after the first world war he had each year gathered a strong team from the United Kingdom and France to play against Oxford during their build-up to the Varsity match. In the 1947 match Stanley's XV included many well-known internationals: Alvarez from France; Bleddyn Williams and Haydn Tanner from Wales; Des O'Brien from Ireland and Vic Roberts, GR Hosking and Micky Steele-Bodger from England. They won the match 15-6.

Our match against Australia was lost 3-5. Australian rugby was not as strong in 1947 as it has since become but the fact that the university side could hold them to a narrow defeat, and Cambridge could hold them to a 9-12 defeat in their match, was an indication of the strength of the university sides of that period. They were probably stronger than in other periods because there were many older students who had seen war service before coming to university. During that period too, an applicant's sporting ability counted a bit more than today in the college's selection process – at least at some colleges.

Oxford was captained by BH (Jika) Travers, an Australian Rhodes Scholar who had made a keen study of rugby. He later wrote a book

Oxford v Australia at Iffley Road, 1947.

entitled *How to play rugby*. He was big, powerful and fast and played eighth man (back row forward). I remember a Leicester defender trying to tackle him when he was under way. Instead of trying to get round him Jika turned towards him, led with his hips and sent him sprawling, without much loss of momentum. Travers had a theory for most situations and very definite ideas on the lines which the forwards should run. His theories didn't carry us through in the Varsity match, which we lost 0-6, but I don't think his theories were to blame. I contributed to the Oxford disappointment by missing a penalty from just outside the 25 yard line, in front of the posts, my kick hitting the left upright. Another South African in the team, Syd Newman, missed three attempts at penalties, but they were from less favourable positions. By contrast the Welsh Lloyd-Davies kicked two penalties for Cambridge from fairly far out and they won them the match.

The University's Michaelmas term ended soon after and in the Christmas vacation the Oxford team went on a short tour to Paris at the invitation of two leading clubs, the Stade Francais and the Racing Club de France. We were put up in a comfortable hotel in the Place de la

Republique and a most hospitable programme was arranged for us by a prominent member of the Stade Francais who was a great friend of Oxford rugby – Serge Saulnier. The day after we arrived we were taken by coach to Saint-Cloud to practise. The following day, a Sunday, we played against Aviron Bayonnais at Parc des Princes and were given a dinner after the game at the clubhouse of the Racing Club. We had a good match against Aviron Bayonnais, winning 20-0. On the Monday we were taken to visit Chantilly Castle and then to a theatre in the evening. The next day we visited Compiegne in the morning and it must have been there that we played against Stade Francais, because we were given a reception at the Compiegne City Hall after the game and later a banquet at the Hotel de Palais.

Our match against Aviron Bayonnais was refereed by Cyril Gadney, probably the most respected referee of the time. He had also refereed our Varsity match and he was soon to referee the match between Australia and France.

In the university's Hilary term, from mid-January to mid-March, the Oxford XV had a lower profile. Fewer games were played than in the build-up to the Varsity match and the clubs we played against were less well known. None of the blues who were to go down at the end of the academic year in June were included in the team.

A match we played away against Gloucester during this period gave us cause for satisfaction. When we arrived at the ground we found a match program which expressed the opinion that the Oxford XV was weaker than the one which had played in the Varsity match but that an enjoyable game could be expected. A further condescending note was struck when our kick-off went straight into touch and instead of taking advantage of a scrum in the middle of the field the Gloucester captain signalled for us to kick off again. The kick had been to the left side and I was standing slightly to the left of the kicker. As he placed the ball for the second time I noticed that our right wing, David Swarbrick, had nobody in front of him and as our kicker walked backwards for his kick to the left I moved up and kicked the ball to the right. The ball jumped awkwardly for Swarbrick but conveniently for me and I was close to the Gloucester 25 yard line before the defence could challenge me. Swarbrick was now running on my inside and I feigned an exaggerated pass to him which stopped the defence sufficiently for me to get past on the outside and score in the corner. After this "sensational" start (as described by the local Gloucester newspaper) we ran out winners by 18-7!

During the Hilary term we also played the inter-college "cuppers" competition which I have already described. Then in the Easter break a strong Greyhound team which included 12 current or future blues toured France and Italy, playing matches at Clermont-Ferrand, Milan, Rome and on the way back Grenoble. We had two managers in Serge Saulnier and Tommy Macpherson, younger brother of GPS Macpherson, one of Oxford and Scotland's great centre three quarters. Tommy played some matches for Oxford although he did not get a blue. He had had an outstanding war record, which included being dropped in occupied France to work with the French underground and he was an ideal person to arrange and manage our tours to France and Italy together with Serge Saulnier. In Italy we received a very warm welcome, which included an audience with the Pope. This proved to be not only interesting but of advantage. Switzerland was offering favourable exchange rates for foreigners coming to the country with travellers

Audience with Pope Pius XII on our Greyhound tour to France and Italy, Easter 1948. Tommy (now Sir Thomas) Macpherson is introducing us. He had mastered basic Italian while a prisoner of war in Italy. In 1943 he escaped while in transit to Germany and got back to England.

cheques. From Milan four of us calculated that we could increase the value of our travellers cheques if we crossed the border into Switzerland, cashed our travellers cheques and then converted the Swiss Franc proceeds to Italian Lira.

We went ahead with our plan but at the Italian border on our way back to Milan the Italian customs officials said our visas for Italy allowed only one entry into Italy, which had been used up, and we could not proceed. Our pleas of youth and ignorance seemed to be having little effect until one of our party had the good idea of showing a photograph of our being received by the Pope. This did the trick and with relief we were able to rejoin the touring party.

Back in Oxford the cricket season was about to start but more overseas rugby was on the horizon before my first year was out: a joint Oxford/Cambridge tour to the Argentine in the summer vacation. In July a touring party of 23 players, 9 from Cambridge and 14 from Oxford, flew out via Madrid to Buenos Aires to stay at the well-equipped Hindu Club and to play nine matches over five weeks, including two matches against "Argentine selections", described in one newspaper as "internationals". We won all of these by reasonable margins. As earlier in France and Italy our university side was warmly welcomed and a number of functions were arranged for us, including receptions at the University of Buenos Aires; at the Hurlingham Club and by the British Legion at the English Club. Eight of our nine matches were played in Buenos Aires, the other being played inland in Rosario.

It had been a very interesting and enjoyable year's rugby.

4

First Oxford Cricket Season

*T*he Oxford cricket season lasted only 3 months because of the long summer vacation but was a particularly enjoyable part of the university year. In my time the university team had a nearly full program of three-day matches at Oxford during the eight weeks of the summer term, mostly against county sides but also including a match against the international team touring England that summer. Then followed a

The cricket pavilion in the Parks, Oxford.

short away tour to two or three counties; a match against an MCC side at Lords; and finally the Varsity match, also at Lord's. With one exception our home games were played in the Parks, a public park with beautiful trees on its northern side and the river not far away to the east. The match which was not played in the Parks in 1948 was the match against the Australian touring team, played on the Christ Church ground in Iffley Road to enable a gate to be taken.

The 1948 Oxford side was ably captained by Tony Pawson, a good batsman who made a lot of runs with his late cut, played later and with a more horizontal bat than the shot which is common today, where the ball is run down to third man with a more vertical

With Hafeez Kardar, who went on to captain Pakistan.

bat turned outwards. Tony was very fast between the wickets, converting many singles into twos. He was also a very good soccer player, a key figure in the Pegasus club side composed of Oxford and Cambridge players which won the amateur cup that year. Eight of the Oxford XI had played in the previous year's game against Cambridge. Philip Whitcombe, the secretary, was a tall and very effective fast bowler. He twice bowled Hutton out cheaply in the match against Yorkshire, and also bowled Hassett in the game against Australia. Hafeez Kardar, a left arm spinner and good left hand batsman, had toured England in 1946 with the Indian team and went on to captain Pakistan after partition. Basil Robinson was a Canadian Rhodes Scholar who bowled off-spinners. Jika Travers, an Australian Rhodes Scholar, had captained the Oxford rugby team the previous season. He

31

was mainly a medium-paced bowler, though he could also make runs. Another medium-fast bowler was Tony Mallett, who later came out to Rhodesia and then to Cape Town, where he was a very successful headmaster at Bishops. It was an interesting team to play in, with a strong commonwealth representation.

Probably because I had played for Western Province before coming up to Oxford I was invited to play in the freshmen's trial match and having made a few runs and taken some wickets was chosen to play for the university. I found myself playing against cricketers I had read about. The counties often rested some of their senior players when they played against Oxford or Cambridge but the matches were still classified as first class fixtures. The Yorkshire side which was one of our first opponents in 1948 included Hutton, Watson, Coxon, Wardle and Brennan, all of whom played for England. We had a good game against them, making 351 in our first innings and bowling them out for 170 in theirs. In our second innings we declared at 144 for 8 but this time they turned the tables on us, getting close to the 326 required for the loss of 6 wickets. When the last over started only 12 runs were needed for victory. But a wicket fell and they only got two of the runs. I made 72 and 42.

In the next match, against Hampshire, we again made sufficient runs to set our opponents

Cricket gear in need of upgrading, pictured during an early game in the Parks: Western Province cap; Bishops jersey; odd batting gloves and well-worn pads.

a target in the final innings, in this case 290 in 2 hours 40 minutes. They fell behind and at the close of play were 187 for 8.

Three of our home matches, against Gloucestershire, Warwickshire and Free Foresters were seriously curtailed by rain and were drawn. Against Gloucester I had my first experience of batting on a sticky wicket. At that time pitches were not covered once play had started and if it rained and the sun came out on a wet wicket it could become sticky and very difficult to bat on. We struggled in making 51 for 8 wickets before play came to an end and I was happy with my contribution of 8 not out! I was awarded my blue after the match, to play against Cambridge.

The Australian team which came to Oxford was without Bradman, Lindwall and Miller but quite strong enough without them: in batting order WA Brown, Arthur Morris, Neil Harvey, Lindsay Hassett, who captained the side, Hamence, Loxton, McCool, Saggers, Ring, Bill

Oxford and Australian teams at Oxford (Christ Church ground) 1948.
The two captains, Lindsay Hassett and Tony Pawson, are seated in the middle.
Hugh Webb and I do not have blues blazers because we have not played against Cambridge.

Johnston and Ernie Toshack. Brown and Morris made 139 for the opening wicket and McCool and Loxton had a good partnership later, enabling them to get to 431. We replied with 185 and 156, which gave them an innings victory with 90 runs to spare. Toshack took three of our wickets in each innings, including mine in the second innings, lbw for 14. In the first innings I got to 32, run out. Kardar made most runs for us, 54 and 29.

Recently I found a description of the match in Jack Fingleton's book on the tour, *Brightly Fades the Don*, including an anecdote about Lindsay Hassett and Tony Pawson:

> "The Oxford skipper, Tony Pawson, was very popular with the tourists. When the pitch was to be rolled at one stage, Pawson asked Hassett what roller he would like. Hassett has a splendid poker face.
> 'What have you got?' he asked Pawson.
> 'There is the heavy, the medium and the light' answered Pawson.
> 'Haven't you got a spiked one?' asked Hassett.
> Pawson looked hard. 'I don't think so' he answered very seriously 'but I'll make sure'. And he went away to ask. Tony was known as 'Spike Pawson' after that."

Apart from the anecdote I was pleased to see that in a book by Fingleton on the great Don Bradman I had got a mention. Fingleton wrote: "Keighley, Kardar, who top-scored in both innings and would have been a leading member of the Indian team in Australia if he had not come to Oxford, and van Ryneveld did well with the bat for Oxford, but the university was badly outplayed. Van Ryneveld was to distinguish himself later as a slow bowler in the University match but he was not known at this stage as a bowler."

The Australians were playing against an MCC side at Lords in their next match and although I knew I was going to watch, hoping particularly to see Bradman bat, I did not feel I could ask one of them for a ticket. When I got to Lords the next day in good time for the start I found to my disappointment that the ground was full and the gates closed. So I never saw Bradman.

Our only win in the Parks was against Middlesex, playing without Denis Compton and Bill Edrich. We made 404 for 5 wickets (Kardar 138) and bowled out Middlesex for 115 and 170. JD Robertson made 59 for them in the first innings and Leslie Compton, Denis' brother, 65 in the second.

On tour we drew with Sussex and Surrey and beat Somerset and an MCC side and came to the match against Cambridge at Lord's in good form. Cambridge had five previous blues in their team, including Trevor Bailey and Doug Insole, and freshman Hubert Doggart, who had made 215 not out against Lancashire at Fenners. Cambridge, batting first, were dismissed for a modest total of 209, Whitcombe taking 7 wickets for 51. We then got 361, mainly due to a fluent 145 by Hugh Webb, batting at number 6. He and Tony Mallett put on 112 for the 8th wicket. Hugh was a natural all-round sportsman, getting blues for golf, squash and racquets in addition to cricket. In their second innings Cambridge were dismissed for 144, not enough to make us bat again. Having taken no wickets in 25 overs in their first innings I hit the jackpot in their second with 7 for 57.

After the game Tony Pawson told me, unexpectedly, that I had been elected captain for the following season. I was unaware that any election was taking place. A long time after I heard that the commonwealth players had swayed the choice!

Postscript. In March 2011 the memorial service to Hugh Webb has just been held. After we were married, Hugh and his wife Jean became close friends of my wife Verity and myself. Jean and Verity had both nursed at St Thomas' Hospital, and Hugh spent his career there after a Short Service Commission in the Army Medical Corps in Singapore and a spell in the Rockefeller Foundation's viral research institute in India. Coming back to St. Thomas' in 1958 he progressed from Registrar in Neurology to Consultant and ultimately to Professor of Neurovirology. He had his own research unit at St Thomas' and his work in the area of viruses in the central nervous system was given recognition by the award of a Doctorate of Science by the University of London. His work brought him to Cape Town more than once and my wife and I saw them regularly on our visits to England, on one occasion playing tennis with them on the indoor court of the All England Lawn Tennis and Croquet Club at Wimbledon, of which Hugh was a member. In 2003 Verity and I watched the two women's singles semifinals in which the Williams sisters were playing from Hugh's seats in the centre court.

In 1945, while captain of cricket at Winchester, Hugh had received an invitation from Field Marshall Montgomery to spend 11 days with him in Germany in that September, after the school year, together with the Viscount's son David, who was also at Winchester. The Field Marshall was then Military Governor, British Zone, Germany. Hugh kept a diary in pencil in an exercise book and in retirement had it transformed into a Journal, complete with copies of Montgomery's personal letters to him, and photographs with him, and also copies of his "Personal Messages from the C-in C" during the final months of the war "to be read out to all Troops". It is a very interesting journal.

The eulogy at Hugh's memorial service was given by Dr Peter Greenhalgh, another very good friend of my wife and myself. Peter had been a merchant banker at Hill Samuel & Co in London but in a change of career came to Cape Town in the 1970s to lecture in classics at the University of Cape Town. By then I had left the bar to join the South African subsidiary of Hill Samuel and heard about Peter's coming to Cape Town both from Hugh and from Hill Samuel in London. Verity and I became close friends of Peter and his wife Mary and among other things in the 1990s stayed with them at a holiday house and smallholding they had bought in Greece, just outside a small coastal village on the mainland Pelion Peninsula, opposite Skiathos. The vegetation there was not unlike the fynbos of the Western Cape. Peter and Mary were by then living back in England. Peter had written a number of books, including a two-volume biography of Pompey and a book on the history and art of the ancient churches and castles of Mani, the area on the very southern tip of Greece.

5

More rugby, for Oxford and England

*I*n little over a month after the combined Oxford/Cambridge tour to the Argentine the new 1948/49 academic year started, with the Varsity rugby match only eight weeks away. Gully Wilson, a second-row forward who would play for Scotland later in the season, was captain, and four players who had come up strengthened the team significantly: Lewis Cannell, a strong-running centre, Murray Hofmeyr, flyhalf (later fullback for England) from Pretoria University; John Kendall-Carpenter, in the front row, big and fast; and Nelles Vintcent from Bishops and the University of Cape Town, a second-row forward who excelled in the lineouts.

Our record leading up to the Varsity match was good, although we lost two matches. We beat Richmond, Leicester, Northampton, Blackheath, Harlequins and Gloucester; drew 0-0 with Cardiff; and lost 0-6 to a strong Queen's College, Belfast team and 9-12 to Major Stanley's XV. Our side included 7 players who were already or were to become internationals.

Cambridge were not far behind with 6 internationals: Barry Holmes, fullback for England; LG Gloag, wing for Scotland; JV Smith, wing for England though in this match playing centre, partnering a New Zealander HM Kimberley, who was captain; Glyn Davies, flyhalf for Wales; Arthur Dorward, scrumhalf for Scotland; and JA Gwilliam,

Oxford XV v Cambridge December 1948.
Back row from left: **Cannell, Gill, Kendall-Carpenter, Kininmonth, Vintcent, Meadows, Wilson, Stewart.**
Seated: **Bridge, my brother Tony, Gully Wilson (captain), Swarbrick, CvR.**
In front: **Green and Hofmeyr.**

second row for Wales. So the scene was set for a keen match, which it proved to be.

Murray Hofmeyr put us ahead with a dropped goal after receiving the ball from a Cambridge "25" dropout. He added to this by making a good break which led to a converted try and before half time we scored another try after a good back line movement, putting us 11 points up.

In the second half Cambridge came back strongly. An article by H.F.E. in *Punch* described the second half in true *Punch* style:

> "Cambridge came very near winning this match in the
> second half. Their three-quarters, it is, I hope, fair to
> say, never looked a very formidable machine, but the
> forwards played a grand game, Glyn Davies broke
> away at last from his escort and ran superbly for a try
> which Holmes converted, and a penalty goal a few

minutes later brought Cambridge within striking distance at 11-8. They struck, too. For what, to this quaint old partisan, seemed an unendurably long time they swooped about the Oxford line in the old familiar way. Smith, at outside centre, made some strong straight runs to support his considerable reputation, Gloag on the left wing came very near making one or two bricks out of remarkably little straw, Dorward and several of the forwards were only held up on the line. Then there was a tragedy – bravely borne in some quarters. One of the Cambridge centres, when in the Oxford twenty-five and, if memory serves, with two men outside him, chose to attempt what looked like a short kick ahead, Oxford's van Ryneveld – not the forward, the other one – got a foot to the ball, kicked it ten yards ahead and found himself in the wide open spaces with only one man to beat, and a perishing long way to go. His subsequent journey has been widely commented on in the Press, and I shall not dwell on it here, beyond remarking that it is a great thing to be young and fit."

There were not many minutes to go after that and we had won 14-8.

Soon after the match my centre partner Lew Cannell and I were invited to trials for the selection of the England team for the first of the five nations matches starting in the new year. The first trial match was at Penzance, near the tip of Cornwall, nearly as far from London as you can get to within the borders of England. It was a pleasant place for a trial match and I would not easily have got to Cornwall without it.

The second trial was at Twickenham. There was rain and strong gusts of wind which I remember for the kicking of Barry Holmes, playing at full back and kicking for touch more often than a full back can do today. He had a habit of giving the ball a stylish little flick as he dropped it on his boot, which ordinarily made no difference to the sureness with which his boot met it but the violent gusts of wind more than once blew the ball off course before his boot got to it, with unintended consequences. However, he survived the trial and played all four matches against the other "nations". Barry had been in the same Oxford/Cambridge side which had toured Argentina the previous summer. His home was actually in Argentina and within a year he was to play for Argentina against France. There cannot have been many instances where a player has played for two countries within 12 months. Sadly he died of typhoid fever only a year or two later.

The team described as "The rest" beat the side described as "England" by 6 points to nil and eight of the former, including Cannell and myself, found ourselves playing for England against Wales at Cardiff Arms Park soon after.

The new millennium stadium at Cardiff is a fine stadium but I doubt whether it can provide the atmosphere which was created at the old Cardiff Arms Park at the start of an international, where a packed crowd closer to the ground got the proceedings going with an inspiring rendering of the Welsh National Anthem. This so motivated the Welsh players that it would have been better if we had not won the ball at the first lineout. Their backs came up very fast and I judged it best to kick a short kick over their heads. This I just managed but not in time to stop Jackie Matthews tackling me two to three yards backwards, a rude introduction to playing against Wales.

With Haydn Tanner at scrumhalf, Glyn Davies at flyhalf, Bleddyn Williams and Jackie Matthews at centre and Ken Jones and Les Williams on the wings, Wales had an outstanding back line. There was also nothing wrong with their pack. They played better than we did and their winning margin of 9-3 could have been bigger. Strangely, they ended the season at the bottom of the five nations table with France, each of them winning only one match.

I must digress here to record an entertaining description of one of the Welsh matches of the previous season written by Wilf Wooller in the rugby section of a book *Wickets, Tries and Goals*, edited by John Arlott. Wilf Wooller was regarded as Wales' greatest centre three quarter of the previous decade and at cricket he also captained Glamorgan to the County Championship in 1948. The match was between Wales and France, played at Swansea in bitterly cold conditions. On the other side of the Swansea field from the grandstand there was only a vast open bank for standing accommodation, behind an iron railing. Early in the match spectators came over the railing to improve their view and others then pushed forward until those in front encroached the touch line. By half time there had been a number of short stoppages in the play to clear a way for the touch judge.

"In the second half", Wooller continued, "it would have been possible for Ken Jones, had he been given an opportunity (which he certainly was not) to have scored a try in the seventh row of the spectators. At one stage play was stopped for six minutes, and it seemed to me that icicles were forming on Cliff Davies's nose as he stood shivering on the field. As a game, the French team well deserved their victory by 11 points to 3. Bleddyn Williams, Glyn Davies and Tanner alone produced flashes of their known brilliant form. But the enormous French pack with the giants Soro and Moga, bulking their mighty sixteen stone each, seemed to paralyse the Welsh forwards. It may be that the French rationing system had given them a greater resistance to the cold, but whatever it was, they stopped and started with the greatest of ease and Wales were lucky that not more than 11 points were scored against them".

We were to come up against Soro and Moga later.

Having lost against Wales, we also lost our second match, which was against Ireland at Dublin's Lansdowne Road. The score this time was 14-5. This was perhaps the best period in Ireland's rugby history, following the Second World War, in which Ireland had not been actively involved. Karl Mullen, their hooker and captain, was a strong leader. He had the incomparable Jackie Kyle at flyhalf and a superb back row in Des O'Brien, Jim McCarthy and Billy McKay.

Ireland opened the scoring with a penalty but we then took the lead with a try under the posts, converted by Holmes. I have a newspaper report on the match by RC Robertson-Glasgow, better known as a cricket writer and correspondent, which described the try in flattering terms:

> "Hall had found touch near the Ireland line on the left. From an ensuing set scrummage England heeled and Rimmer sent out a rather awkward pass but van Ryneveld gathered it and swerved and side-stepped clean through the defence for a great try under the posts".

I think I was helped by the fact that my gathering of the ball was 90% but not 100% clean. In those days a referee could blow the whistle for a knock-on if the ball moved an inch in one's hands and I sensed that defenders had hesitated, expecting the whistle to go. In any event Ireland regained the lead with another penalty and a break by Kyle set up a try, making the score 9-5 in Ireland's favour at half time. In the second half we remained within reach for most of the half but another break by Kyle led to a try by their centre Des McKee, which sealed their victory. Ireland went on to win the 5 nations championship.

After two defeats the England selectors made 6 changes to the team for the match against France at Twickenham, three in the backs and three in the forwards. In the backs Ivor Preece came in for Nim Hall at flyhalf, and as captain; W. Moore was to partner him at scrumhalf; and Dickie Guest was brought in on the right wing. Cannell and I were fortunately retained.

Compared with the way a team is prepared and fitted out for an international match today our preparations in 1949 were somewhat archaic. I still have the letter I received from the Secretary of the Rugby Football Union before the match against Scotland, which took place three weeks after the game against France. It was a stereotyped letter with the necessary details typed in, such as, at the top "ENGLAND v SCOTLAND", followed by the date and time of the game and our headquarters, The Park Lane Hotel, Piccadilly. It advised that I had been selected to play for the "ENGLAND" team (typed in). It continued: "A jersey will be supplied to you, and *must* be returned to me in the Dressing Room directly after the game. WHITE shorts should be worn".

With the letter came an annexure advising that there would be a runabout at the Old Deer Park ground, Richmond, at 3,45pm on the Friday. (BRING SPARE JERSEY & SHORTS); and on the Saturday the coach would leave the Park Lane Hotel (Piccadilly Entrance) at noon for lunch at WINNING POST, CHERTSY ROAD, TWICKENHAM. There would be a team photograph at 2,45pm and the kick-off would be at 3pm (Bring International stockings if already supplied). At 5,30pm the coach would return to the Park Lane Hotel and at 7,15 for 7,30pm there would be a dinner for the teams at MAYFAIR HOTEL, Berkeley Square (Dinner Jacket).

RUGBY FOOTBALL UNION.

TELEGRAMS:
"SCRUMMAGE, PHONE, TWICKENHAM."

SECRETARY:
F. D. PRENTICE.

TELEPHONE: POPESGROVE 1708

TWICKENHAM.
7·3·49.

ENGLAND v SCOTLAND.

at TWICKENHAM   on Saturday, 19th.MARCH 1949

Kick-off 3.0   p.m.

Headquarters THE PARK LANE HOTEL, PICCADILLY

DEAR SIR,

You have been selected to play for the   ENGLAND   Team.

Please let me know on or before 12 · 3 · 49 if you are **able or unable** to play. If you are able to play, kindly let me have answers to the questions on the enclosed form as early as possible. If in any way doubtful of being able to play, please inform me without delay.

A jersey will be supplied to you, and *must* be returned to me in the Dressing Room directly after the game. WHITE shorts should be worn.

Travelling expenses, if any (in detail), connected with the match should be sent to me by Wednesday, 23rd.MARCH. If it is found necessary to stay at an Hotel *en route*, the hotel account *must* be attached to the claim for expenses.

Yours faithfully,

F. D. Prentice.

Secretary.

C. B. Van Ryneveld, Esq.,

Letter from the Secretary of the RFU advising that I had been selected to play for the ENGLAND team (typed in) against Scotland.

At the runabout on the Friday afternoon before the French match I met the new players who had come into the side, including the flyhalf I would be playing outside (Ivor Preece, who also came in as captain) and a wing I would be playing inside (Dickie Guest). I had not met them before. We had no coach or manager and I cannot remember that we had much of a team discussion on tactics for the next day. A great deal was left to one's own initiative. The chairman of the selectors came down to the changing room before the game the next day and encouraged us to tackle hard.

France had not won at Twickenham before but with England having lost their two previous games against Wales and Ireland, they had hopes of a first success. It was not to be. They had a first setback before the game when their flyhalf Terreau withdrew because of injury and had to be replaced and a second setback when their scrumhalf Bergougnan was injured half way through the game and was largely a

ENGLAND BEAT FRANCE AT TWICKENHAM

Preece drops a goal against France. The ball is just through the posts.

passenger thereafter. For part of the second half their flank, Jean Prat, played scrumhalf.

We scored a converted try early on when Cannell at first centre broke past his opposite number and got through to the fullback, Alvarez, with me clear on his outside. Alvarez, expecting him to pass to me, tried to cover both of us but when he moved Cannell beat him on the inside to score under the posts. In the second half France had the wind behind them but failed to get over our line and it was England who went further ahead with a dropped goal by Ivor Preece, our flyhalf. Alvarez replied with a dropped goal for France a few minutes before the end of the game but there was no further score, leaving England winners by 8-3.

I remember France's replacement flyhalf, Pilon, getting loud instructions from his colleagues whenever he got the ball. In the circumstances he did well. I also remember the size of the two French locks, Soro and Moga, quite as big as a Martin Johnson or Victor

Tackling the French wing at Twickenham, February 1949.

Matfield. Until then I had thought that French rugby players were smaller than South African players.

Unlike big rugby days at Newlands, there were no curtain raiser matches before the game. Instead the crowd was entertained to music by the band of the Grenadier Guards.

The teams did not run about the field warming up, as they often do today, but the national anthems were played and the Duke of Edinburgh came out to shake hands with the teams.

Duke of Edinburgh shaking hands with the England team, Twickenham 1949.

At the formal dinner in the evening at the Mayfair Hotel in honour of the French team a toast to the French team was proposed by the Chairman of the Rugby Football Union, to which the French captain Basquet replied and the Chairman of the French RFU then reciprocated by proposing a toast to the English team, to which the English captain, Ivor Preece, replied. There was a further toast to the referee, Trevor Jones of Wales.

In the ten or so games I played for the Oxford XV or the Oxford Greyhounds in France I found the French style of play less orthodox than in England or South Africa. They probed more, and when the player with the ball was stopped there was invariably someone backing him up to whom he managed to get the ball, so that the movement went on.

Some, at least, of the balls we played with in France were different, having more leather panels and being therefore heavier. They were a far cry from the balls used today, which look lighter and easier to handle. They do not get as slippery in wet weather. A disappointing feature to me is that they are seldom kicked with a screw which will curve them more safely into touch, possibly because of their lightness. They seem easier to kick goals with, though the kick from round the corner was not known in my day, making comparison unreliable.

French referees blew harder on the whistle. One referee I remember blew so shrilly to stop the play for a scrum that one thought a penalty was coming. A penalty was heralded by two shrill blasts. I wonder what would have preceded a sending-off.

Our final international of the season against Scotland came three weeks later, again at Twickenham. The Calcutta Cup was at stake, competed for at the annual contest between the two countries, and the result was also important because if Scotland won they would have ended up sharing the top of the 5 nations log with Ireland, while England would then have shared the wooden spoon with France or Wales, depending on which of those two teams lost their final match.

In the England side were three current Oxford players, Lewis Cannell and myself in the centre and John Kendall-Carpenter in the front row. John moved successfully to flank or eighth man the following year. Oxford's captain of the previous year, Jika Travers, was at eighth man. At full back we had Barry Holmes, of Cambridge University. There were also Oxford and Cambridge players in the Scottish side: Gully Wilson and Peter Kininmonth from Oxford and Gloag from Cambridge.

Twickenham could take more than 70 000 spectators at that time, and the ground was full. The match was played on my 21st birthday.

Although Scotland started as marginal favourites, having won two of their previous games to England's one, we had a good day and won comfortably by 19 points to 3.

We were helped by an injury to Scotland's strong-running wing Jackson, which reduced them to an effective 14. Jackson stayed on the field but could not contribute much. He and Scotland's other wing

Evading a weak tackle, England v Scotland, March 1949.

England XV v Scotland at Twickenham March 1949.
Back, from left: Roberts, Kendall-Carpenter, Travers, Matthews, CvR, Holmes, Kennedy.
Seated: Cannell, Hosking, Preece (captain), Guest, Vaughan, Price.
In front: Moore and Steeds.

Smith changed sides a number of times according to which side of the field was deemed more important.

Our first try came just before half-time when one of our flanks, Vic Roberts, broke out of loose play in our 25 and got through to the Scottish fullback. I managed to link with him and get his pass, with no defender ahead of me and our left wing, Bob Kennedy, outside me. Wings being faster than centres I passed to him and no-one caught him. Bob was a Rhodesian. Some years later he came on holiday to Cape Town and we were pleased to get together. He was killed in the conflict in Rhodesia not long after that.

We scored four tries in the second half, of which I scored two. The Times correspondent obviously thought I had made too much fuss of the first because he wrote that I had "dived over the goal-line in the manner of the storybooks". Our last try was a satisfying one because it came from a straightforward backline movement from a scrum or lineout on the left. The ball went smoothly along the line to our right centre Lew Cannell, who beat his opposite number for speed on the outside, ran to their fullback and passed to our wing Dickie Guest running at full speed down the touchline. One seldom sees a movement of that kind today, because the defending backs are lining horizontally across the field and come up too fast to allow four passes.

About this time I received an invitation to play for the Barbarians on their Easter tour to Wales, which I accepted with alacrity.

The Barbarian Football Club was started in the 19th century by William Carpmael, of Blackheath, who conceived the idea of a strong band of players drawn from anywhere in the British Isles touring outlying parts of the country where there was a strong club. In 1890 he organised four experimental games in the North Midlands and later in the year a general meeting was held at which 50 players were chosen to be members and rules of the club were adopted. Carpmael was the Hon. Secretary and Treasurer for the first decade. In 1913 an office of President was created, which naturally went to Carpmael, while another Blackheath member, Emile de Lissa, became the treasurer. He took over as President in 1936 and was President until his death in 1955. His place was taken by another big name in Barbarian history, Jack Haigh Smith ("Haigho") who had been secretary for 30 years, but he unfortunately died within weeks of becoming President and the office went to Brigadier Glyn Hughes, a person with an impressive record in medical and military spheres. During the first Great War he was awarded the DSO as a subaltern in 1916 and a bar a year later, followed by the MC and the French Croix de Guerre avec palme. In the second world war, although now 47 years old, he enlisted again and was sent to France with the Fifth Division. Later in the war, having risen to the rank of Brigadier, he was the chief medical officer in the army advancing on Germany and the first MO to enter Belsen, where he took responsibility for the care of the inmates and the cleaning up of the camp. He later gave evidence at the Nazi War Criminal Trials. For his second world war services he was awarded a further bar to his DSO; the American Legion of Merit; and the Order of St John of Jerusalem. His name was specially revered in Jewish circles.

I regret that when I met him on the Easter tour of 1949 I had no idea of his fine record. I knew him only as a respected member of the Barbarian "support team" consisting, apart from him, of "Haigho", Herbert Waddell, a great Scottish player and father of Gordon Waddell, Jock Wemyss, veteran of the 1914-18 war, Charles Hopwood and one or two others who accompanied us on the tour and among other things selected the teams.

For the 1949-50 season I was asked to be on the committee and from the annual card for that year, on which the current members were listed, I see that the fine Welsh centre Bleddyn Williams was also on the committee, and Micky Steele-Bodger, English flank.

The latter is President now, and has been for some years.

From the start the plan was to play attractive, running rugby and to play it in a sporting spirit. Those principles have remained the guiding principles of the club.

Cardiff was one of the fixtures in the first official Barbarians tour in 1891 and it was an annual fixture from then until very recently, except for the war years. By the 1930's the annual fixture list had settled down to games against Leicester on Boxing Day; against East Midlands in early March, and an Easter tour to Wales, on which 4 games were played in 5 days against Cardiff, Newport, Swansea and Penarth, requiring a touring party of about 30 players. From 1901 Penarth's Esplanade Hotel became the headquarters for the matches in Wales. We were still staying there in 1949 and we were very well looked after by the hotel. Sadly it no longer exists.

The year 1948 brought an innovation; a match against the touring Australian team. The committee was not unanimous in agreeing to the fixture, apparently because of reservations about increasing the number of games the club undertook in one season, but mainly because funds were still needed to cover the expenses of the Australian tour the match was approved. It was played at Cardiff Arms Park before a full house. The committee insisted that the Barbarian team be chosen from the current members of the club, not as one representing the United Kingdom. It consisted of 6 internationals from England, five from Wales, two from Scotland and one from Ireland; and an uncapped player, the Blackheath winger Martin Turner. The brilliant Welsh scrumhalf Haydn Tanner captained the team. The game proved a great success, a fine spectacle of running rugby, which the Barbarians won 9-6, and as a result a match against international touring sides became a fixture.

I watched on television the game between South Africa and the Barbarians late in 2007. South Africa had shortly before won the World Cup in France and had on the first match of their short tour to the United Kingdom beaten resurgent Wales, who were to win the 6 nations competition that season. It was interesting to see that players from Australia and New Zealand were included in the Barbarian team. The South Africans in their World Cup games had had little practice in playing running rugby. Some of them, at least, commendably tried to play running rugby in this game but they were outplayed by the Barbarians.

In 2011, I hear, the Barbarian selectors have gone even further afield in choosing players and have included one from Georgia! I hear too that with the advent of professionalism and changes in club rugby the old programme of matches is no longer possible, including the Easter tour to Wales. But there were matches this year against England and Wales, both won by the Barbarians in the last minute.

Reverting to the tour to Wales in the Easter of 1949, I played in the game against Cardiff, which we won 6-5. The field was wet and quite muddy, making the ball slippery, but I enjoyed in particular playing outside Jack Kyle, the Irish flyhalf, and struck up an understanding with the Irish centre Des McKee, playing in this match on the wing, which the Barbarian selectors thought was his better position. His opposite number decided his best defence against McKee was to shepherd him towards the touch line and tackle him from the side. This he did, but as McKee fell forward he was able to flip a short pass to me backing up on his inside. We didn't score directly from it but twice gained a lot of ground. Another Irishman in our side was the flank Jim McCarthy. Jim was a great friend of Tony O'Reilly and came to Cape Town with him in 2007, when Tony brought international directors of Independent Newspapers for a meeting and a function at Kirstenbosch. My wife and I were very pleased to take Jim and his wife on a drive round the mountain.

Barbarians' Easter tour in Wales 1949.
The row seated is the "support" team, with Glyn Hughes, Emil de Lissa and Haigh Smith in the middle. Sitting on the ground are Micky Steele-Bodger, second from left, Glyn Davies, fifth from left, and Jack Kyle, sixth from left. Bleddyn Williams is fourth from the right in the back row.

6

Cricket Captain – 1949

Although seven of the previous year's team had gone down and Hafeez Kardar and Philip Whitcombe were seldom able to play before they had finished their final examinations, we had a successful season up to the Varsity match, winning 4 games against county sides, including Yorkshire, and also beating the New Zealand touring team – with the help of a very sticky wicket. During this period Cambridge only won one of their matches. Unfortunately they turned the tables on us at Lord's, winning by 7 wickets.

University cricket had the advantage that although one was playing mainly against counties one was not competing in the county championship and not having to think about the team's position on the log. One could therefore more easily make a generous declaration in the hope of a win but with the risk of defeat. In our first match against Gloucestershire we led them by 69 on the first innings and declared with 9 wickets down in the second, 284 ahead. This they nearly achieved, with Tom Graveney making 108, but at the end their last pair had to survive 15 minutes to save their draw – which they did. Fifty-eight years later Tom and I were both in the President's box at Lord's and he reminded me that I caught him with what he generously described as the best catch he was ever out to. He was hitting out and the ball went high over the bowler's head. I ran back from mid-off and dived to catch it as it came over my shoulder. For us Donald Carr made the first of his three centuries in the season and George Chesterton took six wickets in the first innings and three in the second.

We declared in both our innings in our second match, against Worcestershire, making 369 for 6 in the first and 189 for 6 wickets in the second, leaving our opponents to make 227 in three hours. This they did with 6 wickets to spare. I had the compensation of making a century and Chris Winn, who opened for us, made 49 and 95. It was interesting batting against Roley Jenkins, a leg-spinner who gave the ball a good deal of air. He had played in all 5 tests in George Mann's tour to South Africa the previous year and during the 1949 season had the distinction of taking two hat-tricks in the same match, playing against Surrey.

The Yorkshire side which came to play us in the Parks was without Hutton, Watson and Wardle but was captained by Norman Yardley and included two new discoveries in Brian Close and Freddie Trueman. We made a modest 209 in our first innings, Murray Hofmeyr being our top scorer with 58, but they managed only a few more, 222. In our second innings we made 223 (Whitcombe 57) and then bowled them out for 141 to win by 69 runs – a very pleasing victory. Chesterton and John Bartlett each took 7 wickets in the match, and Whitcombe 5. I received a telegram from Sir Pelham Warner the next day: "Congratulations. The last time Oxford beat Yorkshire was in 1896, when I was up".

To my regret I did not keep the telegram, which would be a museum piece on two counts, firstly because telegrams are now extinct and secondly because it was from Sir Pelham, an icon of English cricket. After a lifetime involvement with cricket at various levels, which included playing for and captaining England, being President of the MCC, and writing many books and articles on cricket, the stand next to the members' pavilion at Lord's was named after him, the Warner stand. The first cricket book I possessed was his book *The Book on Cricket* (4th edition). In it I was struck by his choice of the greatest game he played in, a game he lost! He was captaining his MCC side against South Africa in Johannesburg in January 1906. When the last South African batsman, Sherwell, went in on the final day South Africa were still 44 runs behind but Dave Nourse (father of Dudley) and Sherwell hit the 45 runs to win the game by one wicket. Would anyone today choose a test match he had lost as the greatest game he had played in? Sir Pelham was in Lord Hawke's MCC team which came to South Africa in 1898/9. After 22 more years cricket for Middlesex and England he had an exciting last first-class match at Lord's when Middlesex under his captaincy beat Surrey with ten minutes to spare to win the County Championship. He was carried off the field shoulder high and there was a leader in almost every English newspaper the next day to mark his success and his retirement.

We were put in our place by Lancashire in our next match, losing by an innings and 108 runs, but then had an exciting win against the New Zealand touring team under Walter Hadlee, father of the fine all-rounder Richard Hadlee. It was the only match they lost during their tour. England had the better of the test matches but could not achieve a win in the three days for which the matches had been set down. Although Bert Sutcliffe and their best bowler, Cowie, were rested against us their batting was strong with Martin Donnelly, Hadlee, Wallace and John Reid and we would have had little hope against them if we had not had the advantage of batting on a good wicket, after which a thunderstorm and a hot sun made the wicket

Oxford and New Zealand teams in the Parks, 1949. Martin Donnelly is squatting in the front row on the left; John Reid is third from the left; Chris Winn and Donald Carr in sweaters fourth and sixth from the left. In the row behind, Walter Hadlee, the NZ captain, stands between me and the tall Philip Whitcombe.

very difficult for them. Murray Hofmeyr made 95 in 5 hours in our first innings of 247. The New Zealanders had 67 for 3 by the end of the day. On the second day, after the rain, 22 wickets fell for 160 runs. The New Zealanders could add only 43 to their overnight score to total 110. We were then bowled out for 72, of which Chris Winn made 37, and New Zealand lost 5 of their second innings wickets for 45 before the close of play. They held back Martin Donnelly for the third day, when the wicket was expected to be easier, and he and Wallace had an eighth wicket stand of 49, but it was not enough to avert defeat by 83 runs.

We then had wins against Free Foresters, Sussex and Middlesex in the Parks and on tour lost to Warwickshire and Surrey but beat Hampshire and an MCC side.

With our good record up till then, compared with a solitary victory on Cambridge's side, we felt confident going into the all-important Varsity match but were outplayed by Cambridge. Cambridge were captained by Doug Insole and had strong batting. Having won the toss they built up a first innings total of 359, with their first five batsmen all getting runs – Dewes 48, Doggart 60 and Stevenson 70. We made a disappointing 169 in reply and had to follow on. Although we fared better in the second innings, with 322, we could not stop them hitting off the 133 required for 3 wickets with 17 minutes to spare. It was a disappointing end to an otherwise successful and enjoyable season.

Two decisions I made at the beginning of the match failed to produce the result I hoped for. Our team was chosen by Chris Winn and myself and in choosing a wicket-keeper I plumped for Iain Campbell, who was a big hitter – just the person, I thought, to drive home an advantage. Unfortunately he failed to hit any sixes and didn't have his best match behind the stumps. The report on the match in *Wisden* gave us credit for a successful season up to the Varsity match but ended: "In selecting the wicket-keeper for the University match van Ryneveld did not escape criticism. It was generally felt that John Tanner, who played for the university in Association football, was the most efficient, but the vacancy went to Campbell, who, though not so reliable behind the stumps, was more likely to make runs." Quite polite, but a black mark!

The second decision was to start with an extra slip instead of third man for our opening bowlers, Whitcombe and Wrigley, both good bowlers. John Dewes quickly steered two or three balls through the slip cordon for fours and it seemed to give them the initiative.

Today one often sees third man being dispensed with in favour of an extra catcher and I invariably think back to my Varsity match experience at Lord's. I think that dispensing with a third man is overdone.

My disappointment at losing to Cambridge was relieved a week later by getting an invitation to play for the Gentlemen against the Players, a match with a great tradition going back to 1806. In the first half of the 19th century the professionals were stronger than the amateurs and in the middle of the century had 19 successive wins. In 1865 the position changed sharply with the advent of WG Grace, playing as an amateur, although it was no secret that he earned more from his cricket than his expenses. In 1865 Grace was 16 years old and for the next 41 years he dominated the matches and the Gentlemen won most of them. In his last match on his 58th birthday he made 74, the highest score in the match. The amateurs held their own until the outbreak of

The Gentlemen XI v The Players at Lord's, 1949.
Back row from left: Trevor Bailey, Reg Simpson, Hafeez Kardar, CvR, Hubert Doggart, John Dewes.
Seated: Bill Edrich, Freddie Brown, George Mann (captain), Norman Yardley, Billy Griffith. (From *The Cricketer*)

the first world war in 1914. After the war the professionals were generally too strong, losing only four times between then and the match I played in in 1949. The match fell away when the distinction between amateurs and professionals was abandoned after the 1962 season.

The Gentlemen nearly won in 1949. We were captained by George Mann, who had captained England in South Africa on the 1948/49 tour. Freddie Brown, who was to captain England in the last two tests against New Zealand and on the tour to Australia the following year, was also playing and four players from the Varsity match just finished: John Dewes and Hubert Doggart from Cambridge and Hafeez Kardar and myself from Oxford. Others in the side were Bill Edrich, RT Simpson, Billy Griffith and Trevor Bailey. Denis Compton captained the Players, whose team included Len Hutton, John Langridge, Tom Graveney, Godfrey Evans, Close, Hollies and Jenkins.

We made only 105 in our first innings, Hollies taking 5 for 32, and the Players 234, with Close top scorer with 65. In our second we were in trouble at 85 for 5 but Trevor Bailey and I then put on 115 and George Mann followed with 43 for a total of 267. Requiring only 139 to win the Players lost 6 wickets for 69, at which stage we were very well placed, but Godfrey Evans and Roley Jenkins knocked off the 70 to win.

A report in *The Cricketer* described the final day's play:

> "In all its long history Gentlemen v Players at Lord's – which goes back to 1806 –has had few more interesting finishes than this year's match. The Players were set 139 runs to win, but there had been heavy rain during the night and, on a pitch which helped the bowlers, they lost 6 wickets for 69 runs, TE Bailey, pavilion end, and FR Brown, bowling very well indeed, each taking three wickets. At this point Evans and Jenkins, playing with great determination and skill, and running very fast between wickets, in thirty-five minutes before lunch, and one over of Bailey's afterwards, had won the match. Their's was a great effort indeed, but did not FG Mann, the Gentlemen's captain, make a mistake in keeping on Brown for an hour and three-quarters without a rest? The fingers of leg-break googlie bowlers are apt to lose their vitality after, say, an hour's continuous bowling, and strong

as he is Brown was visibly tiring. The best of captains make mistakes – did not Napoleon say the best general is the one who makes the fewest – but on this occasion should not Brown have been rested soon after Evans joined Jenkins, and an attempt made to hold at least one end tight. AH Kardar, from the pavilion end, bowled steadily, but NWD Yardley, a most accurate bowler with the knack of getting out the best batsmen in the world, was not called on, nor was CB van Ryneveld, who with his well-flighted leg-breaks and googlies might well have enticed the batsmen out of their crease or caused them to give a catch in the slips. In both last and this year's University match van Ryneveld had bowled very finely from the pavilion end, and was he not just the type of bowler to induce the gallant, if slightly impetuous, Evans to make a mistake? Changes of bowling however are often a matter of opinion, but one felt that the batsmen were allowed to get set and gain confidence."

The comment that the "slightly impetuous Evans" might have been enticed out of his crease was in retrospect on the mark because he was stumped off my bowling in the Durban test against the MCC in 1957!

The report of the match ended with a general comment: "The match was a great success and has now 'come back into its own'. May it never die out and indeed, why should it?" The match lasted another thirteen years but then fell away with the abolition of the distinction between amateurs and professionals.

I was invited to play in another traditional match later in the season, the festival match between South of England and the touring New Zealand side at Hastings, similar to the Scarborough festival match the following week. I remember the match firstly for playing in the same team as Denis Compton and experiencing his friendly manner at first hand, even to a youngster, and secondly for bowling to Martin Donnelly. I was brought on when Martin was in full flight in a partnership with the New Zealand captain, Walter Hadlee. Martin had played rugby in the same Oxford team as my brother Tony. He could have hit my legbreaks all over the place but for my first couple of overs steered them straight to fielders to give me a chance to settle down.

7

Other Oxford memories

*M*y third year at Oxford was less care-free than the first two because I had spent more time playing cricket and rugby than reading law and needed to reverse the balance. I had written a "law mods" exam at the end of my very first term at Oxford but thereafter there was no exam for two and a half years until my final exams and it had been too easy to defer working for them. Nelles Vintcent was captaining the Oxford XV in the new season and I enjoyed the rugby leading up to the

Oxford v Cambridge at Twickenham, December 1949. Cannell, third Oxford player from the left, has chipped ahead, with Boobbyer and Botting outside him. Ian Botting had played for New Zealand before coming to Oxford.

match against Cambridge in early December, which we won 3-0. I was moved to the flyhalf position, because Lew Cannell was still up and a good new centre had arrived, Brian Boobbyer, whereas we had no obvious flyhalf. I then decided I had to pull out all the stops for the exams and when contacted on behalf of the England selectors said I would not be available for 5 nations matches. That was a poor decision. I also did not play for the Oxford cricket team until after my exams in June. Donald Carr captained the team. In the Varsity match at Lord's Cambridge had slightly the better of the game but it was drawn.

Three good Oxford friends at a rugby reunion dinner: Lewis Cannell, Jimmy Galbraith and Brian Boobbyer. They all paid a visit to Cape Town.

In my third year I could no longer stay in college and went into digs in Merton St, which ran parallel with the High St on the south side of Univ. A convenient lane called Logic Lane connected Merton St with High St and provided easy access to the college. I was fortunate in my fellow students in the lodgings, all at Univ: Nick Gent, John Swire and, for part of the year, Gerald Rothschild. Nick played in the Oxford rugby team and we got together often. I stayed with him and his family one Christmas at Milford-on-Sea and before I left England I was best man at his wedding to Cari ten Bokkel in Holland. He remained a very close friend after I returned to South Africa. John Swire and Gerald Rothschild have also remained good friends throughout our lives. John Swire's family owned J. Swire & Sons, one of the biggest English companies in private hands. Their ships had for many years traded down the east coast of China and they were major shareholders in Cathay Pacific. Gerald Rothschild became a successful diamond agent. He visited South Africa regularly, mostly going to Johannesburg but

Serge Saulnier, left, of the Paris club Stade Francais, organised our Oxford tours in France and Italy. Here Ossie Newton Thomson and I welcome him at Cape Town airport in the 1960s. He was managing a French international team touring South Africa.

also coming to Cape Town, where my wife and I were always delighted to see him. He and his wife Alison had a lovely house in High Wycombe, which sadly burnt down in 2008.

Our landlady in Merton St gave us a good English breakfast. In the evening we had dinner in the college. For lunch I quite often went to Vincent's, a club whose members were almost all blues, having represented Oxford against Cambridge in one or other sport. In my final year I was the secretary, the chairman being Roger Bannister, who a year or two later became the first person to run the mile in under four minutes.

Another person in Oxford who became a close friend was Constantine Trypanis, the Professor of Modern Greek. I was introduced to him by Ossie Newton Thompson, who had met him in the train from London when both of them were coming to Oxford for the first time, Ossie for his Rhodes Scholarship, Constantine to take up his appointment. They quickly struck up a friendship. Constantine and his wife Aliki rented a house in Norham Gardens, just north of the Parks, and were friendly and hospitable. After some years at Oxford Constantine took an academic post in America before returning to Greece, where he was appointed a member of the prestigious Greek Academy and soon after Minister for Education and Culture in the Greek Government. In that post he had responsibility for the Parthenon. He published poetry in Greek and English. Ossie's mother Joyce Newton Thompson, who was Mayor of Cape Town, arranged for

Constantine to give some lectures in Cape Town.

A big benefit from the rugby I played was the travelling which went with it, at minimal personal expense – tours to France and Italy with Oxford and Greyhound sides; the Oxford/Cambridge tour to the Argentine; a trial match for England at Penzance down in Cornwall; and the matches in Wales and Ireland for England. Away matches for Oxford also took one to a number of places in England, through the well-ordered English countryside. If we were playing, for instance, against Gloucester in Cheltenham, we would leave Oxford in a team bus in the morning; stop at a village pub for lunch; get to the ground in comfortable time; play the game; have a couple of beers with the opposition team after it; stop for supper at another English pub on the return journey, and get back to Oxford quite late, having had a very enjoyable day.

My half-section at University College, Nick Gent, getting married to Cari ten Bokkel at the Hague, 1950.

For one away match, against Richmond, we saw little if anything of the countryside. It was misty when we left Oxford and the mist got thicker as we travelled. By the time we reached Richmond there was a thick fog and one could not see far enough to make a game of rugby feasible. We waited an hour or more hoping the fog would lift but it did not and the match was cancelled. Disappointed, we started on our way back. By now the fog was so thick that the bus could only be driven at a snail's pace, a true pea-soup fog. Some of us got out of the bus and walked in front to show the driver the way. Soon we came to the conclusion that we could not get back to Oxford that evening and when we identified a pub we went in and asked the owner whether we could have shelter for the night. He said we could have the sitting room and brought us a big plate of bread and cheese. It was not the most comfortable of nights but an adventure to remember. I never subsequently experienced a fog as dense as that. I think restrictions on the burning of fires reduced the fogs.

I had less travel for cricket. At the end of the summer term the Oxford team played matches away against two or three counties before the Varsity match but the venues were never very far from Oxford or London.

I played a few matches for the Oxford Authentics, the cricket equivalent of the rugby Greyhounds, and one of them was against Winchester College. It was interesting to see a leading "public" school in England after having been to a comparable "private" school in South Africa. Later I was invited there to the wedding in its college chapel of Tony Pawson, who captained Oxford in my first year. At the wedding I met Harry Altham, who was a house master and cricket master under whom many good cricketers learnt their cricket. He was one of the best known people in the English cricketing world, inter alia serving the MCC as Treasurer and later President and being the author of *The History of Cricket*. Hugh Webb and Philip Whitcombe, who played in Tony Pawson's Oxford team, were Wykehamists, and in the Cambridge team Hubert Doggart.

After the end of the Oxford term I played a few matches for another Oxford-related club, the Harlequins, whose members, I understand, had all been cricket blues. The Harlequin colours were a striking combination and the cap became famous (or infamous, in Australia) because Douglas Jardine wore it on his controversial body-line tour. Another club I played an occasional match for was the Free Foresters, perhaps the best-known of the itinerant English cricket clubs, clubs which did not own their own ground. The Free Foresters had a long list of fixtures, all played on their opponents' ground.

Thanks to someone's friendly thought I received an invitation to the annual dinner of the Buccaneer's Cricket Club held at the Lord's Tavern in January 1949 and was privileged to hear a toast to cricket by Sir Norman Birkett, K.C., one of England's most distinguished legal figures. He had first come to the fore as defence counsel in a number of famous criminal cases and had been appointed a judge in the King's Bench Division in 1941. He went on to serve in the Court of Appeal and acted as an alternate judge at the Nuremberg trials. In 1958, having been made a Baron, he took his place in the House of Lords. He was a renowned after-dinner speaker and his love of cricket made him much sought after at cricket dinners. Years later I came across an essay he had written for the 1958 edition of *Wisden* entitled *The Love of Cricket*, reproduced in *The Wisden Papers* (1947 to 1968) edited by Benny Green. The following passage appealed to me:

> "To all lovers of cricket there is a kind of music in the sound of the great names, the sound of Grace and Hobbs, the sound of Trent Bridge and Old Trafford, but the greatest music of all is the sound of the bat against the ball."

Frank Chester, leading post-war umpire, and Denis Hendren, brother of popular England cricketer Patsy Hendren. They enjoyed coming to Oxford to umpire and we benefitted.

Sir Norman also wrote the text for a beautifully-produced book called *The Game of Cricket*, written round a collection of historic cricket paintings. Notes on each of the paintings were written by Diana Rait-Kerr, daughter of the Secretary of the MCC and first Curator at Lord's.

The leading umpire in England during my time at Oxford was Frank Chester. He had been an outstanding batting prospect before the first world war, having played for Worcestershire when he was only 16 and having made a century against Somerset in 1913 when he was 18. Sadly he lost an arm while on service during the war. It was a bitter blow and when it was suggested to him that he should umpire he was at first reluctant to do so but was persuaded, among others, by Sir Pelham Warner. After a couple of seasons umpiring for Hertfordshire Club he applied to be placed on the First-class Umpires List and at the age of 26 became the youngest umpire to stand in the county championship. Within two years he was umpiring in test matches and he became the unquestioned first umpire in England until he retired in 1955.

I got to know Frank because he and another first-class umpire, Denis Hendren, brother of the popular England player Patsy Hendren, seemingly made a point of coming down to Oxford early in each season to umpire a couple of our matches and see what new young cricketers might have come on the scene. They added a good deal to the enjoyment of any of our games in which they umpired.

In 1956, a year after he retired, Frank wrote a book on his umpiring life under the title *How's That!* He had had an unequalled chance to observe first-class cricket. In writing about grounds he said he owed allegiance to his home county ground at Worcester, in the shadow of the magnificent cathedral, and there were many beautiful grounds in England but surpassing them all was The Parks at Oxford!

He regarded Hobbs as a better all-round batsman than Bradman, saying that for all his greatness (which he much admired) Bradman did not have the technique or skill of Hobbs on a sticky or real spinner's wicket.

Among his comments on South Africa's 1935 side which won their series in England through their victory at Lord's he had interesting praise for Jock Cameron: "No wicket-keeper was more popular with the umpires, for he was always fair in his appealing. In the Headingley test Wally Hammond, when 63, made no attempt to play a full-toss from CL Vintcent and was plumb lbw. Cameron and Vintcent eyed each other as if seeking confirmation of a suspicion and some moments elapsed before Jock timidly whispered 'How's that?' I unhesitatingly gave Hammond out." How different from the unrestrained appealing of today!

In my last year at Oxford I was invited to play for the Duke of Edinburgh's side in a charity match to raise funds for the National Playing Fields Association, of which he was Patron. My memory of the game is of a full-blooded shot by Prince Philip into the wide mid-on deep. Many years later at a reunion of Rhodes Scholars at Oxford my wife and my son Philip and I were presented to the Queen and the Duke and I told him I had played for his team in a match at Blenheim. "Badminton" he said. I said I thought Blenheim. "Badminton" he said again. There was no time for more because we were moved on. He was right about Badminton.

My three years at Oxford were enormously enjoyable and interesting and I left very impressed by England.

8

Amateurs and Professionals

*I*n my years at Oxford the separation between amateur and professional rugby was strict and it remained so for many more years. In cricket amateurs and professionals played together in the same sides but they were distinguished in a number of ways. At many grounds they changed in separate changing rooms. At Lord's and other grounds the amateurs and the professionals went on to the field through different gates. When the scores of the county matches were reported in the press the initials of the amateur players were placed before the surnames eg PBH May; MC Cowdrey, but this was not done for the professionals – just Hutton, or Compton.

In playing for Oxford against county sides I cannot remember that I gave any thought to who was an amateur and who a professional. One was concentrating on the cricket. Later I was interested to read a series of articles written by John Arlott in 1949 on the lives of the professionals playing for the seventeen first-class counties. He described how in the main centres of cricket (and almost anywhere in Yorkshire) a fourteen- or fifteen-year-old schoolboy of talent would be watched by the county cricket club and if promising might be offered a post on the county staff when he left school, probably labouring on the grounds and selling score cards, possibly bowling to members. (Denis Compton started that way at Middlesex). With luck he would get a chance to play for the county's second team and work his way up to the first team.

Once accepted as needed for the latter he would get a specific contract, which might take different forms. Some counties paid a salary, either for the summer or for the year, while others paid match money, which could be in addition to a small salary. Unless the player was one of the successful few who were selected to play for England on an overseas tour during the winter his earnings would be modest. He had little protection against injury or loss of form. If he proved himself and was capped he would get a greater measure of security but no guarantee of his future with the county. He could be dismissed at the discretion of the committee. He had no trade union to look after his interests. It was generally accepted that a player would be entitled to a benefit match after playing regularly for a county for ten years but this was also at the discretion of the committee and its value was uncertain. What would he be able to do when his playing days were over?

So why, asked Arlott, did a county pro take up the game as a living? His answer was that the playing of county cricket was a life, not just a living. He would enjoy the playing and the challenge of cricket. The alternative for many would be a humdrum job in office or factory. He would be a local idol, invited to functions and asked for his autograph. He would travel the country as he might otherwise never have done. Arlott concluded: "On a sane and economic level no argument can be adduced for a man becoming a county cricketer: he is valuable to the student of social history only as an example of the incurably romantic – but it is difficult to deny him sympathy, perhaps even envy".

Arlott's series was written in 1949. A significant change took place in that year, when Tom Dollery, a professional, was appointed to captain Warwickshire, the first professional to captain a county side for the season. Warwickshire won the county championship under his captaincy the following year. In 1952 Len Hutton was appointed to captain England for the test series against India. The distinction between amateurs and professionals was also becoming blurred. There were cricketers playing as amateurs on the strength of an administrative position with the county cricket club such as secretary. Other amateurs were generously compensated for "out-of-pocket expenses", sometimes getting as much for their expenses as the professionals were getting for playing.

Tom Reddick in his book *Never a Cross Bat* tells a nice story of being engaged as player-coach for Notts in 1946. At the end of the interview the Chairman, Sir Douglas McCreath, asked him whether he wanted to play as an amateur or as a professional. After a moment's consideration Tom replied: "I am not fussy, Sir Douglas, whichever is the better paid"!

The officially-recognised distinction between amateur and professional cricketers was abolished in England at the end of 1962.

I am not aware of any South African playing as a professional in South Africa during my playing years. One or two had gone to England to play professional cricket, like my uncle Jimmy Blanckenberg in the 1920s and later Stuart Leary, who played cricket for Kent and soccer for Charlton. Eddie Fuller went to the Lancashire League. Basil D'Oliveira was of course another, and other coloured cricketers followed, such as Dik Abed, Cecil Abrahams, Coetie Neethling and Rushdi Magiet. In 1968 at least five of South Africa's best young cricketers were in England in our winter playing county cricket: Barry Richards; Mike Procter; Lee Irvine; Hylton Ackerman and Tony Greig. The five South Africans would surely have been playing on a professional basis, even if their main purpose at that stage was to get experience. In the later part of that season the scheduled 1968/9 MCC tour to South Africa was cancelled and when the 1970/1 South African tour to Australia was also cancelled our isolation from test cricket was confirmed. That changed the landscape for South African cricketers wanting to make cricket their career. There were virtually no opportunities to play cricket professionally in South Africa. After spending the summer of 1970/1 playing in Australia Barry Richards was offered a three-year contract by Natal businessmen to coach and play for Natal but that was exceptional. In the Cape arrangements were made for Eddie Barlow to be appointed marketing manager for Stellenbosch Farmers' Winery and to play for Western Province and soon after, in 1973, he was appointed Director of Cricket Development and also Director of Coaching for the Western Province Cricket Union. He captained the province for ten years and transformed its cricket.

No doubt there were some similar appointments in other provinces but these were few. Unlike the county championship in England there were only a limited number of inter-provincial matches in a season and provinces couldn't afford to pay their players. In the Western Province it was only in the 1978/9 season that the practice of paying cricketers to play was accepted. In that year contracts were signed with four players: Hylton Ackerman, Peter Swart, Allan Lamb and Peter Kirsten. By then the finances of the provincial unions had been improved by the advent of limited overs cricket and by some major sponsorships. SA Breweries had sponsored the Currie Cup competition to the tune of R150 000, spread over 5 years. A Gillette Cup 60 overs competition was organised unofficially by Eric Rowan in 1970 and taken over on an official basis the following season by the SA Cricket Association. Some 5 years later it was replaced by a Datsun Shield Competition. And in the 1980s a day/night series was started, sponsored by Benson & Hedges. At the start Benson & Hedges matches in the Western Province were played at Green Point Common, where floodlights had been installed for soccer, but by 1986 floodlights had been put up at Newlands.

The opportunities for South African cricketers to play on a professional basis were greatly increased when the political scene changed in 1990 with the release of Nelson Mandela from prison and the unbanning of the ANC, ending South Africa's cricket isolation. Today probably all provincial cricketers are paid. In the 2010/11 season 6 players from Western Province were contracted nationally by Cricket South Africa and 14 more had contracts for the Cape Cobras, as the Western Province Cricket Association's franchise team is known.

Judging by the annual report of the Association for 2009/10, Western Cape Cricket is organised on a thoroughly "professional" system described as the Western Cape High Performance Pipeline. Top young cricketers participate in the National Cricket Academy in Pretoria and there is also a Western Cape Cricket Academy. There are winter camps. An Emerging Cobras team goes to Dubai to play in the Emirates Airline ARCH tournament. The report says:

> "Instead of the old well-trodden path of school to club to
> province, early identification and specialised training and
> development are now more important.
> The approach is so professional that only a few franchise
> players even manage to study at university while playing
> today.

A huge (arguably unhealthy) focus, effort and investment is needed if one hopes to reach the top today, both from the player and cricket administrators."

It does seem too specialised.

What will such a player do after his playing days are over? Will his position be much the same as described by John Arlott in his 1949 series of articles on the lives of the professional cricketers playing for English counties? Some, like Kallis, will have earned well and have enough options for their further career but not every player can be auctioned for the Indian Premier League.

9

Mid-Century Writers and Broadcasters

John Arlott in the late 1930s was a provincial police constable and although he had passions for poetry and for playing and watching cricket, the idea of becoming a writer and broadcaster on cricket was beyond his expectations. In a preface to a collection of his writing edited by David Ravern Allen (*The Essential Arlott*) he records: "To find oneself paid for writing verse and reviews and, soon, for watching, writing and broadcasting on cricket, seemed a pipe dream. That feeling was never really overcome: if ever a man was completely happy in his work, this book is a memorial to that happiness".

John Arlott in the broadcasting box at Newlands, 1949.

He got his first chance on the BBC in a programme on poetry and his second in the successful programme *Twenty Questions* of which he was a founder-panellist in 1948. Before long he was invited to broadcast on cricket. According to an article in The Times in 1980 when he retired: "It took a year or two for the public, brought up on Marshall and Swanton, to grow accustomed to Arlott. He did not sound like a member of the MCC. But by 1948 he was established, and ever since has remained, for every test in England, a necessary part of the scene". He combined information on the progress of the game with observations on the players, the spectators and the scene generally and his descriptive ability and rich Hampshire accent made him a favourite with listeners, including many who had not been interested in cricket before.

Arlott got himself into hot water with the BBC in 1950 when on the *Twenty Questions* programme he called the Nationalist government in South Africa "predominantly a Nazi one". There was a diplomatic reaction and he was pulled from the programme for over two years.

Arlott played an important part in enabling Basil D'Oliveira to get to England. Possibly because his antipathy to apartheid became known in South Africa D'Oliveira wrote to him more than once in the late1950s to ask whether he would help to find a way for him to play cricket in England. In a letter written in August 1959 he confided to Arlott that the cancellation of the planned West Indies tour to South Africa to play against non-white sides had dampened his spirits. Bansda and Reddy, co-editors of the South African Cricket Almanack, wrote to Arlott again on his behalf early in 1960, saying he had 80 centuries to his name. Arlott thought the Lancashire League offered the best chance for D'Oliveira to get a position in the English game and wrote to the cricket correspondent of the Manchester Evening News, John Kay. Kay contacted a number of Lancashire League clubs without initial success but soon after discovered that Middleton needed a replacement for the West Indian fast bowler, Wes Hall, who had been forced to withdraw from his commitment to play for them that summer. D'Oliveira was offered the position. Six years later he was an established England player.

Arlott was best known for his broadcasting but also wrote articles for a variety of publications including The Guardian newspaper and the less widely-distributed South Wales Cricketers' Magazine and the

Hampshire Handbook. I have referred in the last chapter to his series of articles on the lives of the professional county cricketers in England and also in a later chapter to his description of the end of the Oval test of South Africa's tour to England in 1951. This appeared in a complimentary article on Athol Rowan which he wrote for *The Cricketer*.

Another success story from an unlikely start was that of Neville Cardus, the most famous writer on cricket of his period. My friend at University College, Gerald Rothschild, gave me a copy of his autobiography when it was published in 1947. Cardus was the son of a prostitute and, so he was told, an Italian musician. He attended a Board School in Manchester, which he described as a place of darkness and inhumanity, and left school at the age of thirteen. He delivered washing for his grandparents, who conducted a home-laundry, and worked for a marine insurance agent, copying out policies. During these years he read widely in the local public library. He became interested in cricket by chance, finding himself outside Old Trafford one day and, on going in, seeing AC MacLaren drive a ball straight and powerfully to the boundary. During that summer of 1902, thanks to the generosity of his aunt, he went to Old Trafford often and he saw Victor Trumper score a century before lunch.

Neville Cardus said cricket opened the door to his becoming the music critic of the *Manchester Guardian*.

In his early 20s he saw an advertisement in a sporting journal: "Wanted Assistant Cricket Coach at Shrewsbury. Must be good bowler. Apply with testimonials." In pick-up cricket and for his club he bowled off breaks, and he applied for the job. He was at Shrewsbury for 5 summers. He became secretary to the headmaster but when the latter was chosen for the headmastership at Eton he could not follow him.

Back in Manchester he was reduced to becoming an agent for a Burial Society, collecting weekly premiums. After a particularly dismal day he decided to write a letter to CP Scott, editor of the *Manchester Guardian*, asking for a job as a clerk, and enclosing one or two specimens of his writing. It brought him a meeting with the editor and in due course, when a vacancy occurred in the reporters' room, an invitation to work there.

For nearly three years he worked first in the reporters' room and later in the "corridor", looking after the back page and writing an occasional fourth leader. In that time he wrote nothing on cricket. While he was recovering from an illness the editor suggested he watch some cricket and perhaps write a report or two. It was 1919 and county cricket was starting again after the war. Initially his reports on cricket were mere additions to his work in the corridor but the following summer he was asked to write on cricket every day, and to travel the country to do so, at an increased salary.

In the years from 1920 to 1939, when war broke out again, Cardus wrote many thousands of words on cricket every week and became famous up and down the land as a writer on cricket. Yet he resisted the description of cricket writer. Cricket, he said, opened his door wide and enabled him to become the music critic of the Manchester Guardian.

He brought to his writing on cricket the command of English which he had acquired in the public library and at the *Manchester Guardian* and his descriptions of the players and their feats gave them and cricket an increased stature. In his autobiography he reproduced a piece on Wilfred Rhodes, great Yorkshire left-arm spinner, which he thought was a special bit of prose:

> "Flight was his secret, flight and the curving line, now higher, now lower, tempting; inimical; every ball like every other ball, yet somehow unlike; each over in collusion with the others, part of a plot. Every ball a decoy, sent out to get the lie of the land; some balls simple, some complex, some easy, some difficult; and one of them – ah, which? – the master ball".

He revelled in the characters of the professionals playing in his native Lancashire and neighbouring Yorkshire, its arch-rival. For instance: "Emmott Robinson was a grizzled, squat, bandy-legged Yorkshireman, all sagging and loose at the braces in private life, but on duty for Yorkshire he was liable at any minute to gather and concentrate his energy into sudden and vehement leaps and charges and scuffles. He had shrewd eyes, a hatchet face and grey hairs, most of them representing appeals that had gone against him for leg-before-wicket".

Cardus was knighted in 1967.

When I bought a newspaper during my time at Oxford it was usually the *Daily Telegraph*, which I found easier reading than the *Times* or the *Observer*. Jim Swanton was its sports correspondent, and a very good one. He lived at Pusey House in Oxford at the time, though often away reporting, and took a special interest in the university's cricket and rugby. He wrote generously of the contribution of South African sportsmen, from Tuppy Owen- Smith on.

Compared with Arlott and Cardus, Swanton was much closer to the cricket establishment at Lord's and viewed cricket from an establishment angle. He had gone to a public school, Cranleigh, in Surrey and his father made him a junior member of Surrey, enabling him to get coaching at the Oval. In due course he was put up for membership of the MCC, fast-tracking the waiting list as a playing member. He was a keen club cricketer and started his own itinerant club, Arabs. He was commissioned to write a series of articles on the sporting histories of the public schools, which brought him many introductions. In 1933 he went on a tour organised by

EW (Jim) Swanton, writer, broadcaster and keen cricketer.

the sporting millionaire Sir Julien Cahn to Canada, USA and Bermuda, which gave him a taste for "cricket travel" and he subsequently organised a number of tours himself with leading players, including one to the West Indies, where he took among others Cowdrey, Graveney, Tyson, and Ray Lindwall, and another to the Far East, taking in Malaysia, Hong Kong, and Calcutta. For the latter he had Gary Sobers, Richie Benaud and Sonny Ramadhin in his touring team.

His first sports reporting was for the Evening Standard, being taken on to their sports staff in 1927 at the age of 20 mainly to write on rugby. In 1938 Harry Altham asked him to collaborate in a second edition of his *History of Cricket*, regarded as the definitive work on the history of the game. In the same year he came to South Africa to do broadcasts for the BBC on Hammond's MCC tour and found himself also broadcasting for the South African Broadcasting Service, the latter's first live broadcasts on cricket. Back in England in 1939 he participated in the first ball by ball broadcasting throughout the day in the tests against the West Indies. The war then intervened and Swanton, having been sent to Singapore, spent three years as a prisoner of war of the Japanese.

In 1946 he was appointed the senior cricket correspondent of the Daily Telegraph and a year or two later also their rugby correspondent. He was also broadcasting on the tests for the BBC, alternating between sound and television. He became the most authoritative writer and commentator on cricket in England.

Jim enjoyed his trips to South Africa in 1939 and again with Peter May's side in 1956/7 but became a strong critic of apartheid and declined to come out with the England tour of 1964/5.

A mid-century writer/cricketer remembered for the quality of his writing and his wit was RC Robertson-Glasgow, known to his friends as Crusoe. While I was at Oxford Jim Swanton gave me a copy of his book *The Brighter Side of Cricket*. On the flyleaf is written, a little grandly, like Jim: "CB Van R from EWS, Easter 1949". I wondered why he chose to give it to me. Its first chapter is headed "Puerilities" and as I paged through the book that seemed the theme, a series of cricket fantasies, often in verse, written with a great enjoyment of cricket, but for me, a keen, ambitious cricketer, not very interesting! Much later I read in Jim's *Follow On* of his regard for Robertson-Glasgow, for his enthusiasm for cricket and "his laugh and wit and unique sense of the ridiculous". He went on: "There never was a party that was not the happier for his presence". Yet he said that a deep private melancholy was seldom far beneath his jesting exterior. Sadly, Robertson-Glasgow committed suicide. Having had four years of depression myself I know how pessimistic one can get. Recently I managed to pick up his autobiography, *46 Not Out*, written in 1948. Crusoe took a classics degree at Oxford, then the highest-regarded degree. He wrote initially for the *Morning Post*, the earliest founded of the London daily newspapers, and, when it closed, for the *Daily Telegraph* and later the *Observer*. As a cricketer he played first-class cricket for Somerset and was invited to play for the Gentlemen against the Players at Lord's. Few first-class cricketers have also written so well.

RC Robertson-Glasgow (Crusoe)

One thinks of CB Fry, who combined classical scholarship and good writing with great cricketing ability. Crusoe could not compare with him as a cricketer but his writing was singular.

Len Hutton, who captained the MCC team in Australia in 1954, listed in his autobiography *Just My Story* the members of the press team who went with them. There were 29 of them! It is interesting to see how many English newspapers then existed with a sufficient readership to warrant sending their own correspondent on a long tour. Among them was John Woodcock, whom I had met at Oxford and who became the respected correspondent of *The Times*. He came to South Africa in 1956/7 to cover Peter May's tour.

In South Africa before the war and for a considerable time after Louis Duffus was the doyen of our cricket writers. He first reported on South African cricket in 1929 when he accompanied the team captained by Nummy Deane to England as a freelance writer. Herby Taylor was the vice-captain and in his autobiography *Play Abandoned*, published in 1969, Duffus described him as South Africa's greatest batsman. In 1931 he was asked to go to Australia with Cameron's team to report for *The Star* and

Louis Duffus

in 1935 he reported on the Springboks' first series win in England under Herbert Wade. Their winning test was at Lord's, where Bruce Mitchell made 164 not out and Balaskas took 5 wickets for 49 and 4 wickets for 31. The other four tests, of three days each, were drawn. Another notable win on that tour was against ever-strong Yorkshire at Sheffield, where Jock Cameron hit three sixes and three fours in an over from Verity. The latter feat is almost better known for the comment of the wicket-keeper than for the feat itself: "You've got him in two minds, Hedley; he doesn't know whether to hit you for four or for six"! Louis accompanied our tour to England under Dudley Nourse in 1951 and continued to write during my playing years.

On the radio front Charles Fortune, who also accompanied the South African team to England in 1951, was our leading commentator for many years. Like Arlott he had a good command of English and enjoyed describing the scene as well as the cricket. Carrying on the broadcast during a stoppage in the play caused him little difficulty.

Jack Nel, who played 6 tests for South Africa as opening bat, tells a story of commentating with Fortune for the first time. Before the broadcast started Charles gave him some guidelines, one of which was "Whatever you do, don't contradict me". On the very first day he was tested. The batsman stretched forward and the wicket was broken. "He's bowled" exclaimed Charles, and invited a comment from Jack. In Jack's eyes the batsman had been stumped and in the light of Charles' guideline he was in a quandary. "Yes I thought so too" said Jack "and its odd that the umpire at square leg raised his finger". The issue was not mentioned further.

I also have a story concerning Charles and the South African Broadcasting Corporation. Some while after I gave up playing Charles asked me whether I would come into the broadcasting box to add comments. It was after play one day in the early part of an MCC tour and I was to join him for the second test at Newlands, presenting myself at the broadcasting box half an hour before play started. When I presented myself Charles told me in a firm voice that the deal was off, as I had not confirmed it. This took me by surprise, as there had been no mention of confirmation, but there was little point in arguing. Many years later Charles confided the ex-

Charles Fortune at the Wanderers, with scorer Laura Knight.

planation. When he had told his masters in the SABC that he had asked me to give comment the latter had told him "he could not have that Progressive in the broadcasting box." At the time Charles had felt it was risky to tell me what had happened. In 2010 we had similar incidents under a different political order.

The writers and broadcasters above were all people I read or listened to for their covering of the live cricket. A renowned journalist of the period whose writing I did not come across at the time was the Australian cricketer Jack Fingleton. He had opened the batting for Australia in the body-line series and in his career had become the first batsman to score four successive centuries in test cricket. Fingleton accompanied Don Bradman's side in England in 1948 as a journalist and went on to write and/or broadcast on every test between England and Australia for the next more than 20 years. He wrote a number of cricket books. In 1972 Sir Robert Menzies, Prime Minister of Australia from 1949 to 1966 and a keen follower of cricket, said he considered Fingleton "the leading writer in world cricket today". He also wrote on the Australian parliament and politics.

From one Australian cricketer/journalist of the period to another: Arthur Mailey was a famous leg-spinner for Australia in the 1920s. While touring England with the Australian team in 1921 he was contracted to do cartoons for the *Bystander* and the *Graphic*. For this the Australian Board of Control relaxed their restriction on players working for a newspaper. He was less lucky a few years later when he wrote an account of a match in Brisbane without having received permission from the New South Wales Cricket Association, who declared him ineligible for first-class matches as a result. By then Mailey regarded his career as a journalist as more important to him than continuing to play. He was one of the writers covering the body-line tour of Jardine in 1932/3 and was less critical of Jardine's tactics than most of his countrymen. Recently I came across his book *10 for 66 and All That* in the library of the Western Province Cricket Club. It is illustrated with his cartoon drawings of leading cricketers and is cheerful reading. My special interest in it is for his explanation of the ballistics of a spinning ball. He wrote:

> "The sensitivity of a spinning ball against a breeze is governed
> by the amount of spin imparted, and if a ball bowled at a
> certain pace drops on a certain spot, one bowled with
> identical pace but with more topspin should drop eighteen
> inches or two feet shorter".

I always felt this was so instinctively but you have to be able to get that extra spin on the ball and you have to bowl a good length to take advantage of it! The latter was always my main concern and in retrospect I don't think that I ever bowled enough after leaving university to develop a sufficiently consistent length. Mailey goes on to say that "a slow bowler who has flight variation depends on variable spin to get that effect. It is not merely a matter of letting the ball leave the hand with more or less impetus". That is taking the science of flight variation to a very sophisticated level. Most of us did try to flight the ball by bowling it "with more or less impetus", bowling it slower or faster, giving it a bit more air or less air, or bowling it from a yard back but I never thought of being able to vary the flight by more or less spin. He also explains that a legbreak bowled with topspin (as opposed to the sidespin of the round arm spinner Clarrie Grimmett) will swerve in the air from the off to the leg before it breaks the other way and a googly or offbreak with top spin will swerve from the leg to the off before it breaks the other way. Mailey's success gives credence to his theory. I wish I had read him earlier but whether I would have been able to get much advantage from his science is another matter!

On the radio and television front the acknowledged master of cricket commentary in Australia was Alan McGilvray. Christopher Martin-Jenkins in his book on cricket broadcasting, *Ball by Ball*, expresses the view that McGilvray, "though less amusing than Brian Johnston, and less profound, literary and emotive than John Arlott, has nevertheless been bettered by no one in the world as a fluent, perceptive and intimate observer of the ebbs and flows of cricket". When Bill Lawry's team team toured South Africa in 1969/70 the SABC commentary team included McGilvray and Johnston.

Alan McGilvray

10

Western Province Cricket Club and Newlands

I returned to Cape Town from Oxford in September 1950, too late in the winter to play any rugby but in good time for the cricket season starting in October. I played for the Western Province Cricket Club, which had two teams in the first division of the league run by the provincial body, the Western Province Cricket Union. From memory the teams in the first division were: Western Province (two teams); Green Point (two teams); Cape Town; Alma; Claremont; Technical College and University of Cape Town. Our matches were played over two Saturday afternoons, starting at 1,45pm and ending at 7pm. We did not play on Saturday mornings because in the 1950s Saturday morning was for many businesses still a working morning. Nor did we play on Sundays in the Cape, though they did in Johannesburg.

I captained one of the two WPCC teams and we managed to win the league in 1950/1. Jack Nel, who had played for South Africa against the visiting Australians the previous year, opened our batting and had a very good season. Another ex-Springbok in the team was Tuppy Owen-Smith, now well into his forties and a busy general practitioner but continuing to enjoy Saturday afternoon cricket. Quite often he was late for the 1,45pm start because he had to finish his medical visits first (in those days doctors still readily went to patients' homes) but we were more than happy to get a substitute to field for him until he came or, if we were batting, to have him bat lower down the order. Tuppy was not only a great all-rounder, having captained England at rugby while studying medicine at St Mary's Hospital, and having made a century before lunch for South Africa at Headingley in 1929; he was also admired for the spirit in which he played. Batting he went for his shots (I remember how he could drive the ball "on the up") and he bowled his legbreaks and googlies with a lot of spin and enviable flight.

It was unusual to have two legspinners in the same team but we enjoyed bowling our legbreaks and googlies. Club cricketers weren't too good at spotting the googlies. I've always thought that legspinning is more fun to bowl – and for spectators to watch – than any other type of bowling.

After more than 50 years it is difficult to remember details of club games but I do remember a decision on declaring. There was an unusual provision in the rules of the first division that if you wished to declare on the first of the two Saturday afternoons you had to do so by 5,40pm. Our wicket-keeper David Graham was an above average left hand batsman but had never made a century and was keen to do so. As 5,40pm approached we wanted to declare but David was in his 90s. With ten minutes to go I sent a message to him that we needed to declare by 5,40 but when that time arrived his score stood at 99. With misgivings I declared, on the principle that the interests of the team came first.

David never achieved a century before he retired and after 50 years I still query whether I took the right decision. Perhaps we should have let him make another run and then proceeded to throw our wickets away!

Although the Wanderers Club in Johannesburg might dispute it, the Western Province Cricket Club was and probably is the best-known cricket club in South Africa, and has a proud history. There is no formal record of its founding but a report in the Cape Argus in 1864 reported that a cricket match was to be played the following day between two teams of "the recently formed Western Province Cricket Club", one chosen from residents of Claremont, Rondebosch and the Diocesan College, and the other from residents of Cape Town and Wynberg. The game was to be played at Southey's field at Plumstead, which had been leased by the club.

Plumstead was in those years far out for most residents of Cape Town and in 1886 the club took a lease on part of the farm Mariendal, in the suburb of Newlands, the site which became known round the cricketing world as "Newlands". Early in 1888 the ground was officially opened with a match between Mother Country and Colonial Born.

Later that year the first overseas team to tour the country, a team from England managed by Major Warton, played their first match on the ground. Major Warton had served as treasurer of the Western Province Cricket Club during a five-year stint in Cape Town with the military and it was through links he had made while here that the tour was organised. There were no South African provincial or national cricket administrations in place in 1888.

In 1890 the Western Province Cricket Union was formed to control the game in the Cape Peninsula and four clubs were admitted to membership at its formation: WPCC, Cape Town, Claremont and Sea Point. Cape Town Club had been started in 1857; WPCC in 1864; and Claremont in 1876.

In the same year an inter-provincial competition was inaugurated, for which a cup was donated by Sir Donald Currie, head of the Union Castle Company. To start with the provincial teams assembled annually at one centre, the initial tournament being only between Kimberley and Transvaal. The first tournament to be held in Cape Town was in 1894, when the teams competing were Western Province, Natal, Transvaal, Eastern Province and Griquas. Newlands was the venue.

In 1895/6 Lord Hawke brought the first of his two touring teams to South Africa and the Cape Town "test match" was played at Newlands. England won by an innings and 33 runs. Lord Hawke toured again in 1898/9. I possess an unusual record of this second tour because Lord Hawke compiled a scrapbook partly of press cuttings and partly of a series of reports written by *One of the Team* at intervals of about a week during the tour. In 1989 I met the Earl of Lindsay, who was Lord Hawke's godson and was visiting Cape Town, and when he returned to England he kindly had the scrapbook photostatted for me. Of particular interest for present purposes is the description by *One of the Team* of practising at Newlands on their arrival:

"Capetown, December 28, 1898.

After our arrival on December 21 our time was fully taken up practising every day on the matting wickets at Newlands, the ground of the premier club of Cape Colony. For the first day or two everyone was at a disadvantage on the matting, our batsmen particularly failing to time the ball. ... It would be hard to find a prettier spot than the ground at Newlands. It is about eight miles by rail from town, and close to the station. The ground, which is surrounded by trees, chiefly fir, has a fine little pavilion perched high up at one end of the ground, with a couple of temporary stands for the anticipated crowd. The view of Table Mountain, which rises up about half a mile away, is simply magnificent, and the plentiful supply of water with the semi-tropical undergrowth make it the most beautiful ground possible to imagine."

Newlands has continued to be Cape Town's leading cricket venue. After initially being leased the ground was purchased by WPCC in 1896 and it was owned by the club for over a hundred years until 1998, when the case for the Western Province Cricket Union taking over ownership became overwhelming. In 1991 South Africa had been re-admitted to international cricket and inter-provincial and international matches had become frequent. The Union (by then re-named the Western Province Cricket Association) was responsible for staging these matches and, not unreasonably, they wanted control of the ground. They had plans for developing the stands and other facilities which required major financing. From the club's side, the frequency of big matches at the ground left less and less scope for the club's matches to be played there. After long negotiations the ground was sold to the Association, except for the members' stand and the area behind it, which remain the property of the club, and with the cooperation of the Cape Town Municipality the club purchased a fine new site a mile away in what was previously Keurboom Park. New state of the art sports facilities have been developed there for the club, with much the same view of the mountain and more trees and less concrete.

Newlands in the 1960s, looking across from the bank next to the scoreboard to the members' pavilion. The public stand on the right was built in 1956.

Members' pavilion at Newlands in the early 1900s.

Lord Hawke's scrapbook entry featured the fir trees round the Newlands ground in 1898. From about that time the firs, or pine trees, along the eastern side of the ground were replaced by oak trees, giving rise to initial adverse comments in letters to the press, but resulting in an Oaks enclosure which became famous.

The matting wickets which Lord Hawke's batsmen needed time to adapt to continued until the late 1920's, when the wicket area was top-dressed with soil from Natal and turf wickets were used for trial games. In 1931, when Chapman's MCC side was here, the Newlands test match was played on turf, the first test match on turf in South Africa. By the time I played there the pitch had become known for being slow and very unhelpful to the bowlers on days one and two. From about the second afternoon it took increasing spin. As a result the toss was an important one to win. I played three test matches there – against New Zealand in 1953/4; against Peter May's side in 1956/7 and against Ian Craig's side in 1957/8. We lost the toss on each occasion. We were forced to follow-on against New Zealand and scarcely managed a draw and we lost the other two tests badly, being bowled out by Wardle for 72 in our second innings against England and for 99 by Benaud and Kline in our second innings against Australia. In later years the pitch was dug up and relaid. My impression is that it has quickened up but it is not a favourite for bowlers, particularly fast bowlers.

The look of the ground has changed a great deal during my lifetime. The view of the mountain on the west side of the ground remains and there is still a bank with oak trees on the east side but elsewhere big concrete stands have been built, including a bigger club pavilion. In the 1930s the ground had little more formal seating than the club's pavilion, the wooden rows of seats under the "Oaks" and a low "stand" on the railway side which was no more than a corrugated iron roof over two or three rows of movable benches. A second team field adjoined the main field, separated by a rope. This has now disappeared from view and from use as a cricket field, replaced partly by one of the new stands and the rest of it by net wickets and parking. Newlands has been given an amended name, Sahara Park Newlands, in deference to an Indian sponsor.

One accepts that things one knew in one's youth have to change but it is nostalgic to think how freely I and my close friends, all keen on cricket, were able to use and enjoy Newlands as junior members before even we were in our teens, and in the ensuing years. We lived within bicycle distance of the ground. There were very good turf nets on the side of the second team field and for some years, as I mentioned earlier, the Chairman arranged for the club coach, Jack Newman, to be available to coach juniors in them in the early afternoons of the Christmas holidays. When he was not there we had nets on our own, keeping strict watch on the length of each's turn to bat. The green box-like scoreboard on the main field had three openings in its face for showing the current innings total and the scores of the two batsmen who were in, with numbers on canvas over rollers which were turned as runs were scored. For the club games on Saturday afternoons we were often allowed to operate the rollers, which involved perching on a narrow shelf. Club games were important then; non-member adults paid a shilling to enter the ground, but we as junior members had free access, and we roamed the whole ground freely, except for the long room, which, as at Lord's, was for senior male members only. A slice of fruit cake was available at sixpence from the tearoom at the back of the Oaks, run by Mrs Creese. She was the wife of the groundsman, Frank Creese, who had taken over in 1925 from his brother WH Creese, who had played minor county cricket in England. When the club secretary resigned in 1938 Frank was appointed to the post of club secretary as well as being groundsman. When he retired his son Ronnie took over his duties of groundsman and caterer, with his able wife Elsa to assist him.

From as long as I can remember the cricket at Newlands had a keen following of coloured spectators. They sat on the sloping grass bank round the south-western corner of the ground called the Willows. Recently I read Peter Oborne's book about Basil D'Oliveira (a unique and fine story) and in it he included Newlands in his sharp criticism of the viewing areas for blacks. He wrote that at the great stadia in South Africa the viewing areas for blacks "were put in the worst positions for viewing and insulated from the rest of the crowd with high wire fences. In Newlands, Cape Town's test ground, the black area was known as 'the Cage' – and it felt like one".

It was not like that at Newlands. The south-western corner of the ground was a good viewing area, closer to the pitch than virtually any other viewing area, and it was not enclosed by a fence. From early on it was partially bounded on the one side by the low railway stand and from 1956 it was partially bounded on the other side by the main public stand and the cordoned-off area in front of the sightscreen. These were "enclosed", for obvious reasons, but not the grass bank between them. In 1973 provision was made for some formal seating on part of the Willows bank and this part was enclosed but the bank as a whole was not enclosed.

In parliament in the late 1950s I was speaking against the Group Areas Act and Paul Sauer interjected "You are not at Newlands now". Paul Sauer deputised for Dr Verwoerd when he was in hospital after being shot and famously made a speech at Humansdorp in which he took a less rigid line on apartheid, only to be repudiated by Dr Verwoerd from his hospital bed. I think Paul Sauer was aware that there was a good relationship between white and coloured spectators at Newlands. There were very few African spectators, mainly because there were then few Africans living in the Western Cape.

The development of the Western Province Cricket Club and Newlands in the club's first century has been well described in the book produced for the club's centenary, *Century at Newlands 1864-1964*, compiled by my uncle, Stewart West, and edited by John Luker. In the period in which I was playing three men, all lawyers, had been and were still prominent in running the club's affairs.

Wally Mars, QC., was the leading trial lawyer of his time at the Cape Bar, a commanding figure in the courts and elsewhere. He played for the club first team for 25 years from 1910 to 1935 and from 1924 to 1948 was Chairman of the club's committee. In 1962 he was appointed President. Until then the position of Honorary President had been held by, initially, the Governor of the Cape Colony and from 1910 by the Governor-General of the Union. When South Africa became a Republic in 1961 the new State President, the Honourable CR Swart, felt it was inappropriate for him to take that position and it was fitting that Wally Mars should become the first member President.

Wally had been responsible for crucial developments such as the purchase of the neighbouring property La Rochelle, preparatory to persuading the Railways to move their alleyway from Camp Ground Road to Newlands station across what is now our south western corner (where the current President's stand is) to a route further south over part of La Rochelle. Again, on the northern boundary of the club was a large property called Kelvin Grove owned by the Rimer family which came up for sale and rather than risk the property being purchased by a developer Wally Mars and his vice-chairman Jim Wiley enlisted the support of sporting enthusiasts and formed a company which bought the property and founded the Western Province Sports Club, a social and sporting club more commonly referred to by the original name of the property, Kelvin Grove. In fact it recently changed its name formally to Kelvin Grove Club. Wally soon became Chairman of Kelvin Grove as well and he was Chairman of both clubs simultaneously for many years. The clubs cooperated closely. The boundary between them was adjusted informally for their mutual benefit, increasing the area for tennis courts for Kelvin Grove and the size of the second team field for the cricket club. Kelvin Grove also had two cricket fields, a small cricket field which was called the Postage Stamp and was used by the WPCC's third team and Friendly XI, and another used by its own club team for its friendly matches.

I have an anecdote concerning Wally Mars which was not recorded in the club's centenary book. The famous English boxer Freddie Mills fought a match in South Africa at the time an MCC team was playing a test match at Newlands and after the bout Freddie came to Cape Town and to the test. It must have been in 1948, when George Mann's side was here. Denis Compton was playing. Freddie apparently knew Denis and he came to the entrance of the members' pavilion and asked to come in to see Denis. The club official at the entrance had instructions only to admit members, so he asked Freddie to wait while he contacted the chairman. He went to the committee bay and told Wally Freddie Mills wanted to come in to see Compton. "Who is Freddie Mills?" asked Wally. "The boxer" replied the official. "Boxer?", said Wally. "No, we don't want boxers in the clubhouse". The media went to town with that story, though I don't think they knew the detail of the chairman's reaction: only that Freddie had been declined entry because he was not a member.

That was more than sixty years ago and I hasten to add that the club is not an elitist club. In particular, in the new South Africa, it has very successfully transformed itself from being a club for white sportsmen and sportswomen to a club for all races.

One year I made a century for Western Province against Transvaal at Newlands and Wally gave me a bat, from his own pocket. The century had a sequel. Fifty years later the Cape Town-born judge in the House of Lords, Lord Hoffmann, was in Cape Town and asked me on what date I had made the century against Transvaal. He had first met his wife at Newlands that day and they wanted to celebrate on the exact 50th anniversary. It was not difficult for me to remember the century, as I made only one against Transvaal, but I couldn't identify the exact date. Ten days later he phoned from London to say he had found it in *Wisden* and he and his wife were about to go out and celebrate.

The second lawyer was Jim Wiley, who became vice-chairman when Wally Mars became chairman in 1924 and took over from him as chairman in 1948, a position he held until 1956. He worked closely with Wally and was involved in all the major developments during that period: the debenture scheme which saved the club from a critical financial situation during the first world war; the purchase of La Rochelle, described above; the formation of Kelvin Grove Club. Jim was a hands-on chairman and ran the club. When I went to the club after work for a net Jim was often there. He was then a partner at the well-known attorney's firm Reid & Nephew, in Cape Town. He lived at St James and like most professional men working in town used the suburban train to go to work. Newlands station was on the way and right next to the ground, so it was easy for him on his way home to get off the train at Newlands, spend time at the ground and catch a later train onwards. It was Jim who arranged for the club coach, Jack Newman, to coach junior members in the nets in the early afternoons of the Christmas holidays.

The third of the triumvirate, Frank Reid, was a King's Counsel at the Cape Bar but his two great interests were the Western Province Cricket Club and the school Bishops. At the latter shortly after the Boer War he was one of the two scholars chosen by Cecil Rhodes to go to Oxford as a trial before he went ahead with his great Rhodes Scholarship scheme which still brings some 75 Rhodes Scholars from the Commonwealth and America (and four from Germany) to study at Oxford each year. He was on the Bishops council for many years and is particularly remembered for building up a union of old boys of the school which has been of importance to the school. At the WPCC, Frank's father JA Reid had been chairman almost continuously from 1896 to 1922. Frank captained the club's first team for seven years and was active on the committee for fifty years from 1910 to 1960. The first matches I played in at the club were vacation matches which he organised for young cricketers on the test match field.

Another Reid, John Reid, not a close relation but a popular member of the club, was responsible for a display of batting which found a place in the club's history. He was a wicket-keeper and though heavily built was quick on his feet and kept wicket with distinction for the provincial side, for whom, however, he batted no 11. In 1949 the Australian side under Hassett was playing against Western Province and Ray Lindwall was bowling fast when John went out to bat. There was some apprehension as to how it might turn out. As he took guard Langley, the Australian wicket-keeper, suggested to him that he should forego a back lift and just keep his bat firmly down in the crease.

This he did and the first ball got a thin edge and streaked through the slips for 4, to the delight of the crowd. The second came down just as fast and another thin edge achieved the same result, to further delight. With eight off two balls John grew in confidence and attempted a drive. This time the edge was thicker, and the ball flew over the slips for another four. The club's history records: "The central figure in this episode maintains that the art of late cutting, which had been out of fashion since the Hammond era, was restored to South Africa".

At the time of the centenary in 1964 fifty-three members of the club had played for South Africa, of whom the most famous was Herby Taylor. Not all played for the club. Jack Cheetham was a member of the club but played for Alma Cricket Club, Gerald Innes and Peter van der Merwe likewise.

The chairman of the committee at the time of the centenary was John Passmore. He was an able club chairman but is most remembered for his work in developing facilities for cricket in two African townships. At the height of apartheid he went into the black township of Langa to see what facilities existed for Africans and finding only a miserable piece of rough ground he raised money and set about developing a proper ground with a pavilion. His achievements deserve a fuller description elsewhere.

The club has over five thousand members today and has been in the hands of a very good committee, chaired by Paul Burton. They have successfully managed the transfer of the club's sporting facilities, of which there are many, to the new site in Keurboom Park; and in the new South Africa they have also, as written above, successfully taken the club from being a club for white sportsmen and sportswomen to a club for all races. When the first team won the local cricket league three seasons ago nearly half the members of the team were coloured or black cricketers. In the 2010/11 season just passed the first team again won the league and it was ably captained by a coloured cricketer, Rushdi Hendricks, and the batting and bowling awards both went to Siya Sibiya, a black cricketer.

Moreover, following in the John Passmore tradition, the club in 2007 launched a Positive Futures Cricket Project, co-funded by UK Sport and the British Consulate General in Cape Town, using cricket as a means of building trust and teaching life skills in marginalised communities. The first project was in Eersteriver, a largely coloured area, and a second project has been started in Khayelitsha, a predominantly black area. The club is well served by its current president, another lawyer, Judge Jan Steyn.

11

With Nourse's team to England – 1951

We went to England by boat, the Arundel Castle. *In front:* Cheetham, Eric Rowan, Nourse and Syd Pegler, our manager. *Up the steps:* Chubb, Endean, Fullerton, McLean, McGlew, Mann, Mansell, Melle, McCarthy, Athol Rowan, CvR and Waite. (From *The Cricketer*)

*I*n February 1951 before the team to tour England was chosen there was a trial match at Kingsmead, Durban, with Dudley Nourse leading the one team and Eric Rowan the other. The wicket was favourable for spin and I took 9 wickets in the first innings of the Rowan XI and 6 in their second innings. I never afterwards managed to bowl with the rhythm I found in that match!

It was more than exciting to be chosen for one's country with the prospect of a six months tour in England ahead, playing on their famous test grounds, and other

Dudley Nourse made 208 with an injured thumb in the first test at Trent Bridge.

county grounds all round England, and matches in Scotland, Ireland and Holland. We went to England in the customary way, by Union Castle boat, taking 13 days. Our team was a mixture of young and old, Nourse, Eric Rowan and Geoff Chubb being over 40, while McGlew, McLean, Waite, Endean, Melle, McCarthy and I were in our early 20's. In between were Athol Rowan, Tufty Mann, and George Fullerton, who had been in Melville's side to England in 1947, and Jack Cheetham and Percy Mansell. Tayfield was called up later when Athol Rowan's knee seemed unlikely to last the tour.

Our tour record overall was not very good, winning only five of the thirty first-class matches, but the test series was close, closer than was reflected by the tally of 3 to 1 in England's favour. We came very close to winning the final test at the Oval and if we had won there the series would have been drawn 2-all.

When the test series started at Nottingham the bookmakers would have given long odds against our winning. We had struggled against the county sides at the start of the tour and two or three weeks before the first test Dudley Nourse had broken his thumb and was a doubtful starter. But we won the test by 71 runs, South Africa's first test victory for 16 years and only our second in England. We owed the win mainly to Nourse's great 208 in our first innings. He batted with a severe handicap because the thumb he had broken at Bristol caused him considerable pain when he tried to impart any power into his strokes.

We batted for almost all of the first two days. Nourse declared when he was out quarter of an hour before the close of play on the second day to have a couple of overs at the English opening pair. The declaration paid off. Cuan McCarthy bowled the first over, which was uneventful, and with a minute to go we ran to our positions to get an over by Geoff Chubb started before 6 o'clock. Cuan was slow putting on his sweater and as he didn't have time to get down to the fine leg boundary he

First test at Trent Bridge, 1951. Cuan McCarthy catches Ikin at leg gully in the last over of the second day. The other fielders are Eric Rowan and Jack Cheetham. (From *The Cricketer*)

stopped at short fine leg. Second ball Ikin turned Geoff round the corner and Cuan caught it. So Geoff got a wicket at age 42 with only his second ball in test cricket and Cuan took a catch at short leg for probably the first and only time in his life.

The catch had a sequel. Our next match was against Northamptonshire and after his catch in the test match Cuan asked if he could field in one of the short positions. He was put at silly mid-on. This time the South African bowlers were taken apart by two left-hand batsmen playing for Northants, an Australian, Livingston, and Jakeman, previously of Yorkshire. They put on 320 in quick time, hitting the ball very hard from the start. Cuan at silly mid-on soon retreated as the balls whistled past him and before long was happy to revert to his more usual positions in the outfield.

Back to the test match, we made 483 for 9 wickets declared. In reply Compton and Simpson made centuries and England got to 419 for 9, when Freddie Brown also declared. He did so because after rain the wicket had become difficult and in the next 2 hours before the end of the fourth day England transformed the game by dismissing 5 of us for 95 runs. When the final day started it seemed we had no chance of winning and might be pushed to avoid losing. This prospect increased when we lost our remaining wickets for 26 runs, leaving England only 186 to get in comfortable time.

Eric Rowan was captaining South Africa in the place of Nourse, who didn't field because of his injured thumb, and he set attacking fields to Athol Rowan and Tufty Mann, who were turning the ball appreciably on the still damp wicket. To our delight, England were all out for 114. The last wicket fell when Johnny Wardle, who had collected a few runs by hitting out, hit an enormous skier off Athol Rowan. Roy McLean was fielding sub for Dudley Nourse on the mid-on boundary and with great confidence, almost nonchalance, took the catch when the ball finally descended.

We had been lucky to make our runs on a good first innings pitch before the rain. In those days the wicket was not covered once the match had started. In our second innings, after the rain, we found Alec Bedser and Roy Tattersall very difficult to contend with. I remember in particular the way Bedser moved the ball off the wicket with his medium-fast leg-cutters. I played and missed many times, fortunately without hearing the off stump rattling behind me.

I was interested to read later in *The Cricketer* of the high opinion SC (Billy) Griffith had of Bedser's leg-cutter. He had kept wicket to Bedser on the tour of George Mann's team to South Africa in 1948/9 and was in a good position to assess it. He wrote:

> "When he bowls it – and herein lies the immense skill – he pitches on a length and invariably makes the batsman play. Noone in my time has achieved to anything like the same degree such a combination of pace, accuracy and length as has Bedser with this particular ball. Admittedly, in the test matches this summer the wickets were generally speaking responsive and often ideal for the leg-cutter to have its full effect ... nevertheless it remains a terribly difficult ball to bowl well. That Bedser took such splendid advantage of the conditions was, to my mind, the highlight of the 1951 cricket season."

Jackie McGlew shaking hands with Princess Elizabeth at Lord's, 1951. Down the line are Waite, McLean, Mansell and myself. Dudley Nourse is doing the introductions.

The second test was played as usual at Lord's. On a fine first day we didn't do badly in dismissing England for 311, bearing in mind they had Hutton and Compton, who had made so many runs against Melville's side, but unfortunately for us it rained overnight on the uncovered wicket. It wasn't a sticky wicket but it was wet and we were not comfortable on wet wickets. Tattersall and Wardle were too much for us and we barely made England bat again. They won by ten wickets.

Our failure on the wet wicket brings to mind England's memorable victory at Lord's against the Australians in 1934, when Hedley Verity took 15 Australian wickets, 13 of them on the same day. England, batting first, made 440, and by the end of the second day Australia had 192 for 2, with Bradman in ominous form. Then it rained and the Australians were unable to cope with Verity, losing by an innings and 38 runs.

As at Trent Bridge and Lord's the weather again shaped the pattern of the 3rd test at Old Trafford. The whole of the Friday, the second day, was washed out by rain and with showers at other times the wicket was damp for most of the match, sometimes justifying the term sticky. It did not favour one side above the other but England had more experience of this kind of wicket and made better use of the conditions.

Having batted at number six in the first two tests I was promoted to batting first wicket down in this test and found myself in the middle before the first over was finished, Eric Rowan having fallen to Bedser off the third or fourth ball. Johnny Waite was also out early with the score at 13, bringing Dudley in. We had a partnership of 51 but thereafter wickets fell regularly and we were all out for 158, Bedser taking 7 wickets for 58. My 40 was our top score. England did not fare much better but an eighth wicket partnership between Laker and Bedser took them past our score and to 211. Geoff Chubb bowled very well for us, ending with 6 wickets for 51.

We made 191 in our second innings, only 138 ahead. On the last morning Hutton batted beautifully, supported by Ikin, in an opening partnership of 121. Ikin was out about twenty minutes before lunch and was replaced by Simpson, with 18 runs to get for victory. Hutton was then close to his century, which would have been his hundredth in first class cricket. With rain pending there was a strong case for them to make sure of their win before lunch but Simpson seemed more concerned with giving Len the strike so that he could get his century. They were still a few runs short at lunch, during which there was another shower, but we resumed on time after lunch and they won by 9 wickets. Len was 98 not out.

The 4th test, at Headingley, was drawn. I made 83 in our first innings, my best test score, and with Eric Rowan put on 198 for the second wicket, which was a record for a South African second wicket partnership and remained so for 30 years. Rowan went on to make 236

Eric Rowan during his 236 at Headingley, 1951.
Hutton at slip, Brennan the wicket-keeper.

and we totalled 538. England however also made a good score. Len Hutton made exactly 100, at which point I bowled him with a ball which was meant to turn but didn't. Peter May, playing in his first test, also made a century and there was no time for a result.

I bowled Hutton in the 4th test at Headingley. Both he and I expected the ball to turn but it didn't.

So we came to the final test at the Oval one match down, still with a chance to square the series. England led us on the first innings and needed only 163 in their second innings to win but it was touch and go before they got there. This was well described by John Arlott in an article he wrote on Athol Rowan for *The Cricketer*:

"England needed 163 runs to win and Nourse, wisely, brought on Rowan early. Hutton and Lowson had made 53 together when Hutton was given out for obstructing Endean as he was about to catch him off Rowan's bowling – a wicket which the scorebook does not credit to Rowan. With the next ball he had May exultantly taken by his brother Eric at forward short leg, and for the last time a scorebook showed 'caught E. Rowan, bowled A. Rowan' – with all that it implies. Van Ryneveld caught Lowson off him at short leg, and England were struggling. They wanted only 79 runs to win, but Rowan and the tirelessly accurate

Athol Rowan turned the ball more than Tayfield.

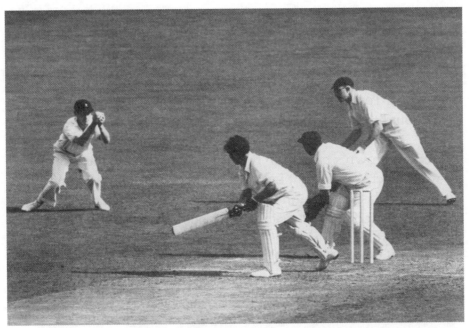

**Catching Compton in the gully off Geoff Chubb at the Oval, 5th test 1951.
Endean is keeping wicket, Mansell at slip.**

Chubb were on top. Two wickets – those of Compton and
Watson – went to Chubb to bring in Brown and Laker, the
last of England's batting of any quality on a wicket which
gave such bowlers the benefit of spin. Both Brown and Laker
played strokes off Rowan which were all but catches to the
leg-trap, and together they lived a nerve-wracking twenty
minutes to tea. When play was resumed the game could have
gone either way.

Athol Rowan, without doubt, knew this was his last match,
and he was of a mind to finish well. Brown, never at his best
against spin-bowling and obviously resolved to lose his
wicket hitting rather than prodding, hit Rowan hard and
high, not particularly safely, but for runs. Nourse took Rowan
off and brought on McCarthy. At once, against fast bowling,
Laker and Brown looked new men, playing firm strokes, and
England moved quickly towards a win. Nourse brought
Rowan back again, but it was too late: physically he had been

finished before the match started; psychologically he was finished when he was taken off in face of Brown's attack. For a few moments the tension was renewed, but the margin was too fine, there was not a single run to play with, and England won a Test which Athol Rowan's bowling had that day brought into hazard".

Freddie Brown's partner in the nerve-wracking twenty minutes to tea was in fact Watson, not Laker (whom one would not ordinarily include in "the last of England's batting of any quality") but Arlott's piece accurately describes the tension. In his book *Cricket Musketeer* Freddie Brown says that before he went out to continue his innings after tea he had a large whisky and soda to give him Dutch courage for his intended hit-or-bust.

He said that when he finally hit Athol Rowan over his head for four Geoff Chubb remarked "Glad to note your bat's got a middle to it"! Freddie got on well with Geoff, describing him in his book as "a great character, always with a smile or a joke whatever the state of the game, a grand chap to have on a side". I agree wholeheartedly with his comment on Geoff.

Hutton's being given out for obstruction in England's second innings was one of those unlikely and unexpected things which can happen in cricket. He went to sweep a ball from Athol Rowan but the ball hit his gloves and bounced up over his left shoulder. Reacting to stop it falling on his wicket Hutton pushed at it with gloves and bat and in the process hindered Russell Endean in his attempt to catch the ball. Dai Davies took only a moment to give him out.

Hutton and Compton were two great batsmen for England to have in their side – and for us to play against. Their personalities and their techniques were very different. I think the description of Len by Doug Insole in his book *Cricket from the Middle* is a good one:

"His batting had a majesty and technical excellence which made it both attractive and successful. Because he was single-minded and sensitive and because his concentration took him away from this earth Len was always a rather lonely cricketer and I found it difficult to get to know him. He would occasionally whisper a word or two of very sound advice in my ear and then slide away before it was possible to get him into conversation. ... Sir Leonard was perhaps not a popular cricketer with the other players but he was greatly respected and he lent considerable character and dignity to the game."

Doug's description of Len confirmed such impression as I could get of him. As a newcomer in the South African team I did not try to talk to Len and he did not have occasion to talk to me, apart from an occasion when he asked me to sign some bats.

Brian Johnston wrote that Len had a dry wit and by way of example recorded Denis Compton having told him that during the Lord's test in 1953 he and Len were facing a terrible barrage from Lindwall and Miller and at the end of an over Len beckoned to him for a mid-wicket conference. Denis thought he had some tactic to suggest but all Len said was: "There must be better ways to earn a living than this" and walked back to face the next over.

In his four years of captaining England Len did not lose a series. Against Australia in 1953 he brought back the Ashes which Australia had held since 1934 and he held on to them when England went to Australia a year later.

For a good description of Denis Compton I like that of Alan McGilvray in his book *The Game is not the Same*:

"If I had to choose a solitary Englishman as the epitome of all that is fine in English cricket it would certainly be that prince of batsmen, Denis Compton. He was the ultimate entertainer, a player of extraordinary ability who complemented his talents with an ebullient nature and a showman's flair. He was film star quality, and England loved him. He was marvellously aggressive, ever willing to jump down the wicket and attack. Compton would rather get out than just hang around. He loved the game as he loved life and he captured in his batting a cavalier spontaneity that was pure joy. Like all great batsmen he did not do everything by the book. He made the delivery suit the type of shot he wanted to play. He would shuffle into position to dictate a bowler's line and the exquisiteness of his timing and the strength of his wrists would reduce the best of bowlers to frustration. He picked up many runs on the leg side with his audacious sweep shot, and his cover drive was uncanny in the way it whistled through the gaps".

Denis was a natural subject for a Neville Cardus description and I include it for its description of Denis and for its picture of England in the year I arrived there to start at Oxford:

"When I returned from Australia to London in 1947, I went straight to Lord's and saw Compton delighting a crowd obviously fed mainly on spam: a worn shabby crowd. But now they sat in the sun, and the strain of those heavy years fell from all shoulders as Compton flicked the ball here, swooped it there, drove it right and left, danced cheekily out of his crease even while the bowler was in the middle of his run .... and his hair became more and more tousled. The crowd sunned themselves as much in his batting as in the beneficent rays that came from the sunny sky. Here, at any rate, was something not rationed, there were no coupons in an innings by Compton. The crowd, young and old, were liberated from worry, apprehension and responsibility. They cheered him on to his century, and they ran his runs for him and with him".

Louis Duffus in his autobiography *Play Abandoned* wrote that our tour was not a happy one. From his perspective perhaps it was not, judging it largely on its results and on the incident at Manchester when Eric Rowan and Johnny Waite sat down in protest on the pitch in response to slow clapping by the crowd. When Rowan was later dismissed and came up the steps on the members' stand a rude remark was shouted at him, to which he replied in even ruder language. In the massage room he gave a forthright interview to a reporter which was given wide publicity. Our manager, Syd Pegler, regarded his action as totally unacceptable and damaging to South Africa's cricketing reputation and felt he should be sent home. The team had a tense Sunday.

Whether Pegler was in contact with the SA Cricket Association at home is not known but Nourse intervened, Rowan signed an apology which was distributed to the press and it was hoped the matter was ended. Temporarily it was, although it had repercussions in South Africa after the tour ended.

In saying that the tour was not a happy one Duffus was probably also aware that Rowan's personality caused some tensions in the team. Earlier it had been a factor in his omission from Melville's 1947 team to England. Dudley Nourse was a steady and quiet leader. Eric was chatty and his brand of conversation and disrespect of convention appealed to some more than to others. In the end it created something of a division in the team.

An anecdote of Eric seems to go down well but also illustrates the point. He was captaining us in our match against Essex at Ilford. For lunch on one of the days of the match the county had gone to considerable trouble to put up a marquee and to entertain us to a more formal meal than usual, with the Sheriff as our host. Eric sat on his right; I was across the table. Eric as always ordered a glass of milk. He then dispatched his main course while the Sheriff was busy with his soup and reached for the cheese, knocking over his milk in the Sheriff's direction. His reaction was hardly an apology. "I'm a bugger for my cheese" he said, with a hearty laugh.

Yet he had guts and he made more runs than anyone else on the tour, with an average of 57 in the tests. I remember his century in the final innings of our match against Leicester, made in quick time with well-judged strokes to win us the match. He was one of *Wisden's* five cricketers of the year in 1952.

For me there was plenty to enjoy in the tour, not least the chance to renew friendships I had made in my three years at Oxford. Having been promoted to batting no 3 after the second test I made my highest first-class score of 150 against Yorkshire at Bramall Lane in Sheffield and batted in that position in the last three tests. With Athol Rowan and Tufty Mann as our main spinners I did not do much bowling, although, as I mention as often as I can, I did bowl Hutton at Leeds. Dudley Nourse liked to keep a tight grip on the game and was disinclined to risk a leg-spinner giving away runs.

I enjoyed the luxury of staying in the Park Lane Hotel, our

headquarters whenever we were playing in London, which was quite often, because we played three matches at Lord's and two at the Oval, and in the Shelbourne Hotel in Dublin, where I had stayed with the England rugby team, and at the Randolph Hotel in Oxford.

Cricket-wise the match we played at Oxford was for me a damp squib, as I did not bat. I thought Eric Rowan, who captained us in that game, could have used a bit more imagination. My close friend Robin Rudd was still playing for Oxford and I gave him one of the bats which Stuart Surridge & Co had generously given me (as also to all our team).

Apart from the bats we also received gifts from factories which we were invited to visit, such as Viyella, who gave us two very comfortable cricket shirts. Simpson's in Piccadilly were keen to advertise their cricket equipment and offered to make us suits at very advantageous cost. I bought a beautifully made double-breasted pin-stripe suit which lasted until well after double-breasted suits went out of fashion.

At the festival match we played at Scarborough against TN (Tom) Pearce's XI, our last match in England, I met Sir William Worsley, who was President of Yorkshire Cricket Club, and was introduced to his daughter Kate. After close of play on one of the days Norman Yardley lent me his Jaguar to drive Kate back to the family seat, Hovingham Hall, about an hour away in the Yorkshire countryside, with its own cricket ground. Kate later married the Duke of Kent. Robin Rudd was invited to the wedding but I was not so lucky.

One evening in London the team was given seats to a theatre show in which Vivien Leigh was acting and after the show we were taken backstage, where she greeted us briefly. Eric Rowan's appreciative remark as she made her entrance does not bear repeating.

On the last night of the Lord's test we were entertained to a dinner at the House of Commons. The toast to the South African team was proposed by no less than the Prime Minister, the Right Hon. Clement Attlee, and the toast to the President of the South African Cricket Association by the Right Hon. Anthony Eden. Other famous names on the list of people attending were Selwyn Lloyd, Harold MacMillan, Sir Wavell Wakefield and Sir Pelham Warner. Thirty-three Members of Parliament attended.

This interest in cricket by leading English government figures and members of parliament contrasted sharply with the position in South

Country house cricket at Hovingham Hall, the residence of Sir William Worsley – former captain of Yorkshire. (From _The Cricketer_)

Africa, where the Nationalist majority had little knowledge of or interest in cricket. They were almost all Afrikaans-speaking and Afrikaners were at that stage not generally interested in cricket. When we collected in Cape Town for the tour, before leaving on the mailship, we were invited to visit the House of Assembly and the Prime Minister, Dr Malan, was asked to meet us, which he willingly did over a cup of tea. He had obviously not been properly briefed because in his friendly speech he expressed the hope that we had enjoyed our tour in South Africa. He thought we were a visiting English team.

The first Afrikaans-speaking Prime Minister or President since 1948 to be genuinely interested in watching cricket is ex-President FW de Klerk, who is a regular guest of the Western Province Cricket Club at major games at Newlands.

FAREWELL DINNER

of the 1951

SOUTH AFRICAN CRICKET TEAM,

on board

R.M.M.V. " WINCHESTER CASTLE "

AT SEA 1st OCTOBER, 1951.

— Menu —

Consommé Royale

Fried Fillets Lemon Sole Colbert

Tournedos of Beef Nelson

Roast Turkey with Ham

Parisienne Potatoes

Green Peas à la Menthe

Combination Salad

———

Sweets

Pouding Victoria

Tivoli aux Fraises

Dessert   Coffee

Before air travel!

110

12

New Zealand tour to South Africa – 1953/4

After our tour to England in 1951 under Dudley Nourse I was admitted to the Cape Bar. There was no office available at 4 Wale St, where most of the advocates had their offices, but I got one in Parliament Chambers, in Parliament St, where five or six other advocates had taken offices. Within months the team to tour Australia and New Zealand the following summer was being chosen and I was contacted on behalf of the selectors to check availability. With hindsight I should have jumped at the chance of a tour to Australia and New Zealand but having started a practice I thought it would be unwise to go away for 6 months, and said I would not be available. Even an indication that I would be chosen as vice-captain to Jack Cheetham did not persuade me to change my mind. In retrospect it was a poor decision. I could easily have started at the bar a year later.

As it happened I would probably not have been fit to go on the tour because during the preceding winter, playing rugby for Villagers against Stellenbosch, I was heavily tackled (a little after I had passed the ball) and dislocated my hip. I had a long spell on crutches and on the doctor's advice did not play rugby again.

Jack Cheetham's team did very well, drawing the test series against Australia two-all and winning both the tests they played against New Zealand. Their fielding was outstanding and with its help Tayfield took 30 wickets in the Australian tests. On the batting side Endean's 162 in the second test proved match-winning and the same could be said of McLean's 81 and 76 not out in the final test, squaring the series. In New Zealand Jackie McGlew made an undefeated 255 at Wellington, which broke the South African record for an individual test score then held by Eric Rowan with his 236 at Headingley in 1951.

The New Zealand team which toured South Africa the following summer was the first New Zealand team to tour South Africa. It was captained by Geoff Rabone. He had toured England in 1949 in Walter Hadlee's team, and was now one of only four survivors of that team, the others being Bert Sutcliffe, John Reid and Frank Mooney, their wicket-keeper. In the match against Oxford in 1949 Rabone had taken 5 wickets in our first innings and 6 in our second.

In South Africa they lost four of the five tests, the other being drawn, but the series was not as one-sided as that tally suggests. In the draw at Newlands New Zealand had much the better of the match, making 505, dismissing us for 326 and enforcing the follow-on, and apart from the 4th test, when Rabone could not play through injury and we won by nine wickets, the other tests were well contested.

The second test in Johannesburg was a very dramatic one. We were playing at Ellis Park, better known for rugby, because the old Wanderers ground had been expropriated for Johannesburg railway station and the new Wanderers ground was not yet ready. The pitch was very lively. Cheetham won the toss and we were 259 for 8 wickets at the end of the first day. Endean made 93 and I made 65. I had bruises on my legs from the bowling of Tony McGibbon, who was tall and got lift from the pitch. I did not possess a thigh pad.

The events of the second day started in the early hours of the morning when the New Zealand manager received a cable telling him of a train disaster in New Zealand in which Bob Blair's fiancée had been killed. At the ground the flags flew at half mast and there was a somber mood. Blair did not field. Our last two wickets fell quickly but New Zealand then struggled against Adcock and Ironside on the lively pitch. Adcock's bowling was lethal, rising sharply and hitting gloves and body frequently. Sutcliffe did not open, as he usually did, in the hope of getting the worst of the new ball over before he batted but Rabone and Chapple were out for 1 and 8 and he came in at no. 4. He

**Sutcliffe batting in the dramatic test at Ellis Park
after being felled by Adcock.**

had faced only two balls when Adcock got one to fly, hitting him on the ear and felling him. Helmets had not yet been invented. He was helped off the field. Reid was also hit by Adcock and had made only 3 when he fell to a very good catch by Endean. Miller then came in but was soon hit on the chest and coughed up blood, also being led off the field. Poore was out to Adcock with the total at 35 and although 19 year-old Beck, playing in his first test, and Mooney saw the side through to lunch, only 41 runs had been scored for 4 wickets down, two batsmen injured and taken to hospital, and Blair an unlikely starter. It looked as if the match might collapse. But we were in for a surprise.

After lunch the wicket was less lively. When Beck was out for 16 Miller came out to continue his innings, to an ovation, and he and

Mooney steadied the innings until he was bowled by Ironside for 14. Then Sutcliffe walked on with his head heavily bandaged and received a tumultuous reception from the crowd. He quickly gave notice of his intentions by sweeping Ironside over the square leg boundary for six, followed by a similar shot for four. Soon after Cheetham brought back Adcock at the one end and Tayfield at the other and Sutcliffe hit the latter for three sixes in the first over, saving the follow-on in the process. The 50 partnership between Sutcliffe and Mooney took only 39 minutes. Mooney was out at 138 and when McGibbon and Overton were dismissed and nine wickets were down we thought the innings was over and were beginning to move off the field when Blair unexpectedly came out of the pavilion, to a further warm reception from the crowd. He and Sutcliffe added another 33 valuable runs in 10 minutes. In one over Sutcliffe hit Tayfield for three sixes and Blair added another, the over yielding 25 runs. Tayfield had Blair stumped soon after, leaving Sutcliffe at 80 not out. It had been a marvellous display of batting.

Our lead on the first innings had been reduced to 84 and we made only 148 in our second, so New Zealand required 233 to win. It seemed well within their reach when Rabone and Chapple gave them a steady

Jack Cheetham hitting catches before the Newlands test against New Zealand.
The public stand behind the sightscreen was only built two years later.
The catchers are Waite, Westcott, Ironside, Murray, Endean, McGlew, McLean, CvR, Tayfield (hidden) and Adcock.

**John Reid in the 3rd test at Newlands,
playing a typically powerful drive.**

start but Adcock again took wickets and they were all out for 100, giving us victory by 132 runs.

The New Zealanders were very unlucky to lose Rabone through injury before the 4th test. He broke a bone in his instep playing against Border and was out for the rest of the tour. He had played a captain's innings of 107 in the first test and was one of the three batsmen the New Zealanders relied heavily on, the other two being Sutcliffe and Reid. Reid made 135 in the third test. McGibbon was their best bowler, taking 20 wickets in the tests. Reid took 12 wickets. He was a fine all-rounder. He was strongly built and I remember in particular his shots through the covers off his back foot, hit with tremendous power.

When he came back to South Africa in 1961/2 as captain of the next New Zealand side he made more runs than any other batsman had achieved in a South African season and in the tests topped the New Zealand batting and bowling figures.

In 1953/4 the only centurion on our side was Roy McLean, who made 101 in the first test. Endean came close with 93 in the second, made on the lively Ellis Park wicket. Jack Cheetham made a valuable 89 at Newlands when we were under severe pressure. Jackie McGlew ended up with the most runs in the series, 351, and with the benefit of two not out innings I had

Adcock took 24 wickets in the series.

the best average of 46.80! Adcock took 24 wickets and Tayfield 21. I took 10.

There was a very easy and friendly relationship between the two teams. Describing the second test in his book on the tour, *Silver Fern on the Veld*, RT Brittenden wrote:

> "If there is one other aspect of this game to be considered before proceeding to its day-to-day fluctuations, it is the extremely happy relations which existed between the opposing teams. Perhaps for the first time in recent history, the two teams stayed at the same hotel; they dined together, they went out together, they were the firmest of friends, and if there was not a single member of the South African side who was not extremely popular with the New Zealanders, the same applied in the reverse".

13

Currie Cup – 1955/6

We were lucky to steal the trophy from Natal and Transvaal, who had stronger sides than us. Natal had won the Cup the previous season and had seven Springboks available to them, including McGlew, McLean, Goddard and Hugh Tayfield. Transvaal had four top Springboks in Endean, Waite, Adcock and Heine. All those players had been to England the previous winter in Jack Cheetham's side. In our Western Province team only Eddie Fuller had been to England the previous winter, playing in two tests. Dick Westcott had played three tests against the New Zealanders in 1953/4 and I had had two series against England in 1951 and the New Zealanders in 1953/4.

Our first three games were home games at Newlands. In the first we beat Transvaal by 61 runs. Heine took 5 of our wickets in each innings and for us Jimmy Liddle, a left-arm spinner, took 10 wickets, 7 of them in their first innings. Russell Endean made a fine 91 not out in their second innings, putting on 60 or 70 runs with Dave Ironside for their last wicket before Eddie Fuller trapped him lbw, to our relief.

In our second match, against Eastern Province, we were behind on the first innings but bowled them out cheaply in their second innings and won by four wickets. Against Natal we made 401 in the first innings, thanks mainly to a remarkable146 by a young left-hander Hugh Roy, who swept Hugh Tayfield to the legside boundary for umpteen fours. Tayfield had three fielders protecting the legside fence but Roy went on hitting fours between them. Tayfield ended up with 5 wickets

The Western Province team which won the Currie Cup in 1955/6.
Back row from left: Siedle, Maile, Low, Roy, Pithey, Pothecary, Fuller.
Seated: Westcott, Pieter van der Bijl (Chairman of the selectors), CvR,
George Crichton (Manager), Innes.
Front: McDonald and Ferrandi. *Inset:* Liddle.

but they cost him 170 runs and a good deal of swearing! Natal were 74 behind on the first innings and when we declared with 9 wickets down in our second innings it left them 278 to get in 140 minutes. They sportingly went for the runs, even when they were losing wickets, and fell short by 69 runs. Our club centenary book *Century at Newlands* gave more praise to Natal than to us, saying they were the better side!

In our return matches at away venues we were again behind on the first innings against Eastern Province but won by 41 runs. Then we lost badly, by an innings, to Natal at Pietermaritzburg and needed to win the last match in Johannesburg to win the competition. We suffered a setback before the match when Jimmy Liddle, who had taken most wickets for us till then, had to return to Cape Town for medical

**Signing an autograph, wearing a Western Province cap.
In our day we played for a province, not for a franchise.**

attention. Sadly he was found to have cancer and he died a few months later, aged only 28.

The match in Johannesburg was at Ellis Park because the new Wanderers ground was not yet ready. We knew from the match against the New Zealanders the year before that the pitch was lively and for fast bowling we had only the medium-paced Eddie Fuller, while Transvaal had Adcock and Heine. Our prospects seemed thin. Fortunately for us there was drenching rain before the match and the wicket was still very wet when play eventually got under way, which cancelled out Transvaal's Adcock/Heine advantage. They bowled their normal length and it was too short on the wet wicket. We won the toss and put them in. Eddie Fuller ordinarily relied on swing for his wickets but could also by way of variation run his fingers over the ball for a fastish off-break. This became his stock ball on the wet wicket and he bowled Transvaal out for 81, his own tally being 7 wickets (their first 7) for 40 runs. We scarcely improved on this with 91, of which I managed to get 39. In their second innings the wicket was drier but Fuller again bowled well and they were all out for 129, leaving us to get 120 to win. This we did by the slender margin of two wickets, a very exciting match. Ken Viljoen presented us with the Currie Cup immediately afterwards.

14

Peter May's MCC team in South Africa – 1956/7

M.C.C. Team, South Africa, 1956/7

Front Row: T. E. Bailey,   D. J. Insole (VICE-CAPTAIN),   P. B. H. May (CAPTAIN),   F. R. Brown (MANAGER),   D. C. S. Compton
Middle Row: H. W. Dalton (MASSEUR),   J. B. Statham,   P. J. Loader.   M. C. Cowdrey,   A. S. M. Oakman.   J. C. Laker,
F. H. Tyson,   G. Duckworth (SCORER & BAGGAGE MASTER).
Back Row: B. Taylor,   J. H. Wardle,   G. A. R. Lock,   J. M. Parks,   P. E. Richardson,   T. G. Evans.

*I*n 1955, Jack Cheetham had led the 11th South African team to England, with Jackie McGlew as vice-captain. After 4 tests the series had been even but England won the final test at the Oval to go 3-2 up.

The MCC's return visit to South Africa in October of the following year was warmly welcomed. The last England team to visit South Africa had been George Mann's team in 1948/9, eight years before.

For me it was a bonus that Peter May was captaining the side and Doug Insole was vice-captain. Doug had captained Cambridge in the 1949 Oxford/Cambridge match at Lord's when I was captain of Oxford and Peter May and I had played against each other in the Varsity match of 1950. Of the other players Trevor Bailey and I had had a century partnership in the Gentlemen v Players match at Lord's in 1949. All South Africans were delighted that Denis Compton was in the team, after uncertainty because of his suspect knee.

After a warm-up game against a Country Districts side at Paarl their first provincial match was against Western Province at Newlands, a traditional starting point for tours. They won this comfortably by an innings, Peter May scoring an impressive 162. He was to make centuries in four of his next six innings leading up to the first test – against Eastern Province, Rhodesia (twice) and Natal. Fortunately for us he did not reproduce this form in the tests.

Peter May drove the ball beautifully. (From *The Cricketer*)

The first test was at the Wanderers, starting on 24th December. Cheetham had retired and Jackie McGlew had been appointed captain but on the morning of the match he withdrew because of an injury to his shoulder and I was asked to take over as captain. I had not toured with Jack Cheetham's side in England the previous year and although I had played with six of our team when New Zealanded toured here two years before, I had not played with the other four, including two of our bowlers, Heine and Goddard. It was quite challenging going into a test match knowing so little about one's bowlers and with no time to plan. I asked the bowlers to set their own fields. Luckily Bailey, Compton and May got out early and the cautious batting of Richardson and Cowdrey gave me time to settle in. At the end of the first day England were only 157 for 3, a very slow day's batting. But their partnership of 121 set up their win. England led us by 53 on the first innings and although they made only 150 in their second we were bowled out for a miserable 72 in our second innings, Bailey taking 5 wickets for 20 runs. The Wanderers wicket assisted movement off the seam and Bailey made full use of it.

If the batting was slow in the first test, the scoring rate in the rest of the series was not much better. Over the five tests the average rate per hour was only 32, England a fraction of a run better than South Africa. The main reason for this was that the bowling on both sides was a good deal stronger than the batting. England could pick from Statham, Tyson, Bailey and Loader for quick bowlers and from Laker, Lock and Wardle for their spin attack. On our side we had four outstanding bowlers in Adcock, Heine, Goddard and Tayfield, with some leg-spin available from me if called for. The series maintained its interest for the spectators mainly because they had had little international cricket to watch in the preceding years and because South Africa made a good comeback after England had won the first two tests. Today's spectators would not have come in numbers to see such slow cricket.

The second test followed soon after at Newlands, starting on New Years day before a full holiday crowd, increased by the erection of a temporary stand on the second team field at the Kelvin Grove end which took 5000 spectators. McGlew decided to play, though not fully fit, and resumed the captaincy. Peter May won the important toss. After a steady start by Richardson and Bailey the crowd was entertained to attractive batting by Cowdrey (101) and Compton (58), and a carefree 62 from Godrey Evans, enabling England to total 369. We only managed 205 in reply, Wardle taking 5 wickets. May did not enforce the follow-on and Cowdrey and Compton were again top scorers in England's second innings, which May declared closed at tea-time on the fourth afternoon with 6 wickets down and a lead of 384. This was a good deal more then they needed because Wardle skittled us out for 72, taking a further 7 wickets. His figures in the test were the best of his career.

Among the fast-falling wickets there was that of Endean given out for handling the ball. Laker was bowling and Endean padded up to a ball wide of the off stump. It hit his boot and jumped up above his head. Endean was an international hockey player and probably by hockey instinct parried the ball with his hand. The appeal was slow in coming but when it came Umpire Costello at once gave him out. By co-incidence Endean had also been involved in the other unusual incident at the Oval in 1951, described earlier, when Len Hutton was given out for obstructing him in his attempt to make a catch.

We had a break of three weeks before the 3rd test at Durban. Shortly before it McGlew told the selectors he was not sufficiently fit and I was again asked to take over the captaincy. I think McGlew said at the same time that he would not be available for the further tests. I had told the selectors at the start of the tour that I was to be married a few days after the third test and would not be available to play in the 4th or 5th tests but I was now asked to stay on and to captain the side for the rest of the series. I was happy to do this, although it meant reducing our

We were married at George between the 3rd and the 4th tests, 2nd February 1957.

honeymoon at Plettenberg Bay to three or four days in order to get to Johannesburg for the 4th test. In compensation my wife was invited to fly with me to Johannesburg at the expense of the SA Cricket Association to watch the match. She was not however invited to stay with me at the team hotel and spent the rest of our honeymoon staying with my good friend of Oxford days, Robin Rudd, and his wife Alison.

In the 3rd test at Durban Peter May for the third time running won the toss and elected to bat. Richardson and Bailey had a good opening partnership of 115 but the remaining batsmen failed to capitalise on it and England were all out for 218. We also got off to a reasonable start but it was McLean coming in at no 5 who ensured a lead on the first innings, hitting a century. Roy was often uncertain in the early stages of his innings but once his eye was in he could transform a game and here on his home ground he got on top of the bowling, playing some powerful strokes, and with the help of 19's and 20's from partners got us to 283, a lead of 65.

In the couple of hours left for play on the third day Richardson was bowled and Bailey took a crack on his right hand from Heine which proved to have broken a bone, although he stayed at the wicket until the end of the day's play. Compton and May went out cheaply the next morning and at that stage England had barely eliminated their deficit on the first innings and in the process had lost three of their best batsmen and Bailey had a broken finger. We were in a promising position. Doug Insole rescued the situation for England, making his first test century and holding us up until shortly before lunch the next day, the fifth and last.

We had just over four hours left to get 190. This was above the average scoring rate in the series up to then but the wicket was still good and 190 was not a big ask if we didn't lose too many wickets. Unfortunately that was what happened. Pithey was bowled in the first over and we lost 3 more wickets, including McLean, before the total reached 50. Endean and Funston then gave us a chance with a partnership of 75, but were both out with the total at 124, leaving us to get 66 runs in 35 minutes, with Waite and myself the last of the recognised batsmen. We decided that if we went for the runs at the rate required we were more likely to lose the match than to win it and we settled for a draw.

This was a disappointing result after being in a good position to win but we had at least regained some confidence after being bowled out for 72 in each of our second innings at the Wanderers and at Newlands.

For the first time in the series we won the toss and batted in the 4th test at the Wanderers. The pitch was a good batting wicket, easier than in the first test, and we made 340. Goddard and Waite had a century partnership and McLean followed with 93 before, unfortunately, being run out. I was at the other end and no doubt deserved some of the blame but not as much as the crowd thought. Roy was in very confident mood, coming down the wicket to the spinners, sometimes scoring, sometimes going back. This time he came down the wicket and turned the ball to leg and his call was an ambiguous grunt. I thought it was a no but Roy came on, and in quick time it was too late for him to get back. It was a very unfortunate mishap because we had put on 58, our innings had passed the 300 mark and we were headed for a big first innings total.

In reply England made 251, May getting his highest score of the series, 61. So we had a lead of 89 but 3 days of the test had gone. In the second innings we tried to force the pace so as to have a chance of bowling England out a second time but May set defensive fields and our aggression brought us no more than 142. There was just time to get Bailey caught at short leg off Tayfield before the end of the day and that left England 213 to get on the last day with 9 wickets in hand. We had six hours to bowl them out.

England batted to win, not to draw the match, and with Insole and Cowdrey putting on 82 to take the total to 147, they needed only 85 more with 8 wickets still standing. Goddard broke the partnership, having Insole caught at slip, and that proved to be the turning point. May was out for a duck and Compton for 1, both to Tayfield. Wardle came in ahead of Godfrey Evans and went on the attack, scoring 12 off Tayfield in an over, and he and Cowdrey put on a valuable 30 before he was out swinging at a wide ball. Cowdrey now went on the attack, coming down the wicket to Tayfield and driving with all his weight. The ball went waist high at Tayfield's middle. It went like a bullet but Tayfield held it. And he took the remaining wickets with England just 17 runs short. It was an exciting win. Tayfield took 9 wickets in England's second innings, bowling throughout the last day.

The South Africa XI v England 5th test at Port Elizabeth, 1957.
Back row, from left: **Funston, Pithey, Adcock, Upton (Manager), Heine, Goddard, Duckworth.**
Seated: **McLean, Tayfield, CvR, Waite, Endean.**
Insets: **Watkins, McGlew, Keith, Taylor.**

The Fifth test wicket at St George's Park, Port Elizabeth, on which both cricket and rugby were played, proved to be quite unfit for test cricket but nevertheless provided a close and therefore exciting finale. In advance of the game the pitch had been replaced with turf from a practice wicket, lifted sod by sod. Notwithstanding the good intention it hadn't settled well. When we looked at it the day before the game started there were already a number of wide cracks. These were reduced by watering overnight but as the pitch dried the cracks opened again and when the ball hit them it did unpredictable things, mainly shoot along low.

England had to go into the test without Statham and Wardle, both suffering from injuries, and Compton's knee was suspect. We won the toss, which was valuable, but lost half our side for 78. Endean and I then put on 65 to take the score to 143, Endean getting what proved to be a match-winning score of 70. We were all out for164. For England Bailey and May had a partnership of over 50 for the third wicket, the best England partnership of the match. When they had gone, only Lock of the remaining batsmen got into double figures and England were all out for 110. Adcock and Heine each took 4 wickets. So we had a lead of 54 on the first innings, which was more than useful in a low scoring game. In our second innings we struggled to 130. Tyson was the most successful of the English bowlers. He reduced his pace for the sake of accuracy, relying on the pitch to assist him, and took 6 wickets for 40.

England therefore had 189 to make in the final innings, which would have been the highest total of the match, with the cracks in the wicket getting wider. May was the batsman who gave us most reason to worry, particularly when he went on the attack against Tayfield, hitting him for six over the long-on boundary, followed by a lofted 4 over mid-wicket and 13 off the over. Fortunately for us he received an unplayable ball from Goddard soon after, the ball coming in sharply, presumably off a crack, and hitting him low on the pad in front of the stumps. England had obviously decided that attack gave them the best chance. Bailey was caught in the deep. Cowdrey likewise attacked Tayfield but snicked one on to his pad and I caught him in Tayfield's leg trap. I had to dive but it came quite softly. Compton and Insole went cheaply and the match seemed as good as over. But not without a fight from Evans, Lock and Tyson, who put on 57 in good time, hitting out. I was starting to worry that we were being undone at the last and considered bringing back Adcock and Heine but Tayfield in the end got Lock and Loader and we won by 58 runs. Tayfield finished with 6 wickets for 78 – and a record 37 wickets in the series.

Hugh Tayfield, a very accurate, determined and successful offspinner.

Catching Cowdrey off Tayfield, 5th test at Port Elizabeth, 1957. The others in the picture are Endean, wicket-keeper, Doug Insole, backing up, and umpire Marais.

In retrospect we were lucky to draw the series. England beat us decisively in the first two tests, while the margin was much smaller in the two tests we won. By the end I think Peter May's side were feeling the effects of what had been a long tour – 22 matches in all, coming on top of a summer at home against Australia. In the last test they were without Wardle and Statham, who with Bailey were their most successful bowlers on the tour, and Loader and Compton were both suffering from injuries.

According to a biography of Trevor Bailey, written by Jack Bailey, who was Secretary of the MCC in the 1960s, we were also lucky with some umpiring decisions which went in our favour. It seems Trevor was quite certain that on two occasions, the first during the 3rd test at Durban and the second during the 4th test at the Wanderers, he was given out caught in the leg trap off Tayfield when the ball had hit his pad but not his bat. The umpire in each case was Basil Malan. I caught the ball in Durban and Russell Endean caught him in Johannesburg.

When I caught him in Durban I was in a square leg position in the leg trap and was quite unable to judge whether he had hit the ball. I can't remember where I was fielding when Endean caught him in Johannesburg; I think at midoff. On that occasion too I could not judge whether he had hit the ball, which is often the case when bat and pad are close together, but I was happy that the umpire had thought so. In retrospect, as we won the latter test by only 17 runs, the decision could well have made the difference between winning and losing!

Recently a DVD titled *Cape Summer* was made on the tour for the MCC library by Michael Burns showing footage taken from television, then in its early stage in South Africa, and from the cine camera of Trevor Bailey. The commentary is largely from Peter Richardson and John Woodcock, interviewed by Christopher Martin-Jenkins. Both were complimentary about the tour but Peter Richardson referred to poor decisions against them in the Durban test. It is to the credit of the MCC that, as far I can remember, they kept their criticisms to themselves. The series was played in a good spirit.

There was an incident in the first test at the Wanderers which exemplified this. Denis Compton was batting to Tayfield and drove the ball back to him just off the ground. Tayfield caught it right on the ground and from where I was standing, not far away at short leg, I was uncertain whether he had taken a clean catch or whether the ball had hit the ground first. Denis just asked Hugh whether he had caught it and when Hugh said he had Denis walked. Many years later I read in a book by Doug Insole that the English players believed the ball had hit the ground well in front of Tayfield's hands. We heard no complaint from them at the time.

It is often said that the person who knows best whether a catch has been cleanly taken is the catcher. In my view it is quite easy for the catcher to be mistaken. I think a person watching from the side is in a better position to judge. Today the decision will often be made by a third umpire with the benefit of replays from cameras, which is much more satisfactory.

In Michael Burns' DVD, Peter Richardson records that the MCC team received generous hospitality on the tour, often being invited to parties at private homes. My wife remembers that the teams were invited to the Saturday evening dance at Kelvin Grove Club during a match at Newlands and she danced with Denis Compton, who "danced with a lovely natural rhythm". We did not play on Sundays in those years.

I doubt whether South Africa has ever had a better pair of opening bowlers than Adcock and Heine. Both were tall and fast. Adcock had a beautifully fluent run-up and delivery of the ball. Heine was less fluent but when he got to his delivery stride he gathered his considerable strength and delivered the ball with all his might. His body language was all menace and if he managed to hit the batsman it encouraged him. He did not like to be taken off. Adcock was more accepting of being asked to take a rest. Trevor Goddard normally came on as our first change, to take advantage of the ball still being fairly new. A left-arm medium-paced bowler, he bowled over the wicket, directing his attack mainly at the leg stump with at least one short leg, quite fine. He was a model of consistent accuracy, moving the ball a bit both ways, and batsmen found him very difficult to get away. For spinner we had Tayfield, one of South Africa's most successful bowlers of all time. He did not spin the ball as much as Athol Rowan but used subtle variations of speed and flight and, like Goddard, bowled with great accuracy, never giving up. With Goddard and Tayfield able to keep the batsmen quiet for long periods, we had time to rest Adcock and Heine and bring them back for effective second and third bursts. In the five test matches Tayfield took the most wickets, 37, a South African record for a series. The other wickets were divided fairly equally between the others – Adcock 21; Heine 18 and Goddard 15. I took 4 wickets, including the wicket of Doug Insole twice, in part compensation for having lost the Varsity match to him at Lord's in 1949.

Of our batsmen only Roy McLean made a century. He changed the course of a game when he made runs because he played forcefully and took the initiative from the bowling with his aggressive shots. His century at Durban put us in a position to win, although we did not do so in the end, and his 93 at the Wanderers in the 4th test also put us on top and was as important in our win as Tayfield's 9 wickets in the second innings. Unfortunately he was an uncertain starter and four times in the series did not get into double figures. Our most consistent batsman was Trevor Goddard, who made a few more runs in total than McLean and headed our batting averages with an average of 33, a very valuable all-rounder. Johnny Waite was another valuable all-rounder as wicket-keeper batsman. He was quite slim and lanky and not the quickest between wickets, but there was nothing wrong with the quality of his strokes or the speed of his wicketkeeping. Russell Endean had a disappointing series by his standards but his 70 in the final test at Port Elizabeth was invaluable, twice as much as anyone else on our side. He also kept wicket in that match, after Johnny Waite was injured, and did so very competently. In 1951, when Dudley Nourse's team for England was chosen, Russell had been chosen as the first wicket-keeper but Johnny Waite had batted well and been preferred. In that series Endean had also taken over as wicket-keeper in the last test following an injury to Waite. Russell and I shared hotel rooms often in that 1951 tour and he was my closest companion in all the games I played for South Africa.

15

Australians in South Africa – 1957/8

Australian team in South Africa 1957/8.
Back row from left: Favell, Grout, Simpson, Meckiff, Drennan, Mackay, Klein, Jarman.
Seated: Norton (Manager), Burge, Benaud, Harvey, Craig (Captain), McDonald, Davidson, Burke, McLennan (Baggage Master).

We had ended the series against Peter May's side the previous season on a high note but were brought down to earth by the Australians. Although we had the better of the first and third tests we failed to clinch a win in either of them and we lost the other three. With hindsight I was too bold to make myself available for the series, as I had recently been elected to parliament and had a lot other than cricket on my mind. Commitments in my constituency, East London, resulted in my having very little cricket before the matches against the Australians started. I remember buying a newspaper from a young coloured newspaper seller at the top of Adderley St. after the team for the first test had been announced. Without any introduction he said: "Jy's nie fit nie"!

I did get 53 in the Western Province match against them but injured my hand and had to withdraw from the team for the first test in Johannesburg.

In the first test Jackie McGlew and Trevor Goddard had a great opening partnership of 176 and Johnnie Waite also made a century, enabling us to declare at 470 for 9 wickets. Heine then took 3 Australian wickets cheaply and they were 62 for 4 but with a century by Benaud, batting no 7, they recovered to 368, limiting our lead to 102. There was then insufficient time for a result. In the fourth innings they achieved a draw comfortably with only three of their wickets down.

I lost the toss at Newlands, which gave the Australians the big advantage there of batting first. As noted earlier, the Newlands pitch was in those days an easy batting wicket at the start but later took spin. McDonald and Burke put on 190 in their opening stand and Australia totalled 449. We then batted poorly against the spin of Benaud and Kline and lost by an innings. In our second innings we were bowled out for 99. This not only put Australia one test ahead in the series but made a dent in our confidence which contributed to our failing to press home our big advantage in the next test.

At Durban we dismissed the Australians for 163, Adcock taking 6 wickets for 43 runs. Although we lost two early wickets, McGlew and Waite then had a partnership of 231, each of them making a century. They batted with great determination, after our collapse in Cape Town, but very slowly. McGlew took over nine hours to reach his century, longer than Peter Richardson had taken for England at the Wanderers the previous year and in fact longer than anyone in test history. As our lead increased the wily Australians didn't hurry with their overs. Our total of 384 put us 221 ahead with ten hours to play. Having no hope of winning, the Australians played for a draw and they managed that with a little bit to spare. At the end they were 71 runs ahead with seven wickets down.

We might have won this game if we had not given Neil Harvey a reprieve after he had been run out. He had turned a ball towards the far fine-leg boundary, with Tayfield in pursuit. Hugh and the ball got to the boundary at the same time and from the way he picked the ball up I and others got a clear impression that it was a boundary. Hugh was a great competitor at all times and to us his slow pick-up and turn indicated that the ball had hit the fence. The batsmen got the same impression and being near the end of their third run started to walk back to their original ends. Tayfield then threw the ball back and shouted that it was not a four and I was easily able to take off the bails with Harvey still out of his crease. I didn't immediately appeal and Trevor Goddard, who was nearby, said "Surely we can't get him out that way." Instinctively that seemed to me the right reaction and I decided not to appeal. Our generosity cost us dearly, because Harvey kept us at bay for at least another hour and made 68. When we left the field at the next interval Ken Viljoen, who was our manager for that match, was anything but pleased, saying we weren't playing village cricket. He was no doubt right, as Harvey should have waited for the umpire to signal a four before walking back to his wicket, but having thought about the incident many times I mostly don't regret our decision. Cricket was a game, with an enviable reputation for fair play. Ian Craig came to our changing room immediately after the game ended and expressed his appreciation.

In the recent (July 2011) test at Trent Bridge, Ian Bell was given a similar reprieve by MS Dhoni after leaving his crease before the ball was dead. On the strength of the television replays and Bell's own explanation, he had less justification for assuming the ball had gone to the boundary than Harvey had in the Durban incident. Bell said "we thought it was probably four, with the way the fielder reacted after he got up". On that basis Dhoni's gesture was more than generous. It would be interesting to know on what basis Andrew Strauss and Andy Flower approached Dhoni. The latter's decision was however well received and cricket's reputation for fair play underlined, even if the incident was not without its queries.

I had the satisfaction of bowling Richie Benaud in the Durban match, and getting Bobby Simpson caught by Tayfield. I enjoyed bowling on the Durban pitch.

Australia beat us convincingly in the 4th test at the Wanderers. We had the misfortune to suffer a chapter of accidents. Heine had a damaged ankle, though he was still our most successful bowler. Adcock was off the field for a considerable time with flu. Johnny Waite injured his hand and I did the same, splitting the webbing of my hand and having to have five stitches. Australia made 401 in the opening innings, Benaud scoring his second century of the series. We only managed 203 in reply and when we followed on we were out for 198. Australia needed only 1 run to win the match and the series.

We fared little better in the final test at Port Elizabeth. Roy McLean had had a poor series and was dropped in favour of Peter Carlstein. We made 201 and Australia replied with 291, "Slasher" McKay making their top score of 77. In the second innings Davidson and Benaud each took 5 of our wickets and our 144 total meant they only had to get 68 in the final innings, which they did for the loss of 2 wickets.

The final innings was not without interest because for an unexplained reason the wicket became very lively and Adcock and Heine bowled extremely hostile overs, the most hostile I ever saw. Three short balls from Adcock went perilously close to McDonald's head and soon after he snicked another to Tayfield in the slips. Grout and Harvey were also peppered with rising balls and the umpire spoke to me, asking me to ensure that the bowlers pitched the ball up. After another over from each I switched to Goddard and Tayfield. Apart from the umpire having taken a hand I had throughout the series asked Adcock and Heine to limit the number of bumpers they bowled to an average of one per eight ball over. The incident at Ellis Park against the New Zealanders, when Bert Sutcliffe was hit on the head by Adcock and taken to hospital, had made a considerable impression on me. Batsmen didn't have helmets. Australia only needed another thirty or so runs and a barrage of short balls at this juncture was not appropriate.

In *Cricket Exiles*, a book written by Brian Cowley, I found the following description by Charles Fortune of those overs by Adcock and Heine:

"When Australia needed no more than 68 to win the St George's Park crowd was treated to the most terrifying eruption of fast bowling I have ever seen.

The light was drab and the evening chilly. Heine and Adcock between them sent down seven overs of electrifying pace and soaring trajectory. Adcock in his first over gave Colin McDonald three successive bumpers all of which missed him only by hairbreadths. Then both umpire and skipper van Ryneveld called for a stop to this style of attack. Adcock promptly sent down the daddy of all bumpers. From it McDonald was caught at slip.

Later than night, about 1am, I bumped into Neil and Piet, still very 'stroppy' and quite unrepentant! As bowlers maybe they had had their fill of bowling in a side that would make no runs to supplement their own prodigious labours."

I think they were also frustrated at the limit I had placed on their bumpers during the series. In retrospect we could legitimately have used more.

16

In Parliament

Between the tours of Peter May's MCC side in 1956/7 and Ian Craig's Australians in 1957/8 I was persuaded by Zach de Beer, my close friend from school days, and Sir de Villiers Graaff, Leader of the opposition United Party, to stand in a parliamentary by-election at East London. I had been at Oxford when Smuts unexpectedly lost the 1948 election to the apartheid policy of the Nationalist Party headed by Dr Malan. Worrying apartheid legislation ensued: the Group Areas Act; the Population Registration Act; the extended Immorality Act; the Separate Representation of Voters Act, intended to remove the coloured voters from the ordinary voters roll. In the 1953 general election I canvassed for Zach de Beer, standing for the United Party in the Maitland constituency, which he won. He was only 24 years old but an able speaker in both English and Afrikaans. As in 1948 the United Party won a majority of votes in the country overall but the Nationalists increased their majority of seats in parliament.

A few months before the 1958 general election was due the United Party MP for East London North, Herman Malcomess, died. At de Beer's suggestion Sir de Villiers Graaff, recently elected leader of the United Party, invited and persuaded me to stand. He said it was a safe United Party seat which would probably not be contested.

In the event Donald Woods was nominated to contest the by-election by the Federal Party, which had a following in Natal. Its policy on racial issues was marginally more liberal than that of the United Party but it

138

was known mainly for its strong support of South Africa's British connection. Donald and I were not at daggers drawn. Half way through the election he rang me and we had a drink together. Later we also found ourselves canvassing the coloured voters on the same evening. There were not very many of them and our paths crossed more than once. It was the last election until 1994 in which coloured voters voted on the same roll as white voters. Donald's Federal Party made little headway against the official opposition party and I was elected by a big margin.

Only six months later the 1958 general election was held. On this occasion I was opposed by a Nationalist, Robbie de Lange, who had been mayor of East London, but my majority was again comfortable. East London was 1820 settler country, conservative on race issues but English-speaking.

I was not quite 30 years old when first elected and I had recently married Verity, daughter of the Anglican Bishop of George, Bishop John Hunter. We could live in our home in Cape Town for the six months parliamentary session but for the six months recess moved to my constituency in East London, where we rented a house as best we could. This half-yearly move was not easy. Our eldest son Mark was born in 1957 and our second son Philip followed in 1959. From a family point of view losing my seat in 1961 proved a relief. Our daughter Tessa was born the following year.

The four years during which I was in parliament were eventful political years. Soon after the 1958 election the Prime Minister Dr Strydom died and was succeeded by Dr Verwoerd, who had been Minister for Native Affairs. In the latter capacity he had appointed the Tomlinson Commission to make recommendations for the development of the Bantu (African) homelands, and based on its report Dr Verwoerd now outlined his vision for ensuring that the white people of South Africa retained control of their destiny. He accepted that a policy of white baasskap (supremacy) in the whole country could not succeed indefinitely and therefore proposed that the Africans should exercise their voting rights separately in the reserves set aside for them. There were to be separate homelands for each of the ten ethnic units making up the Bantu (African) population. He said that these "could even develop to being independent homelands". The Act which set this course was The Promotion of Bantu Self-Government Act 1959.

A later family photograph. Mark and Philip were very young during my years in parliament and Tessa was not yet born. We moved to my constituency in East London each 6 months recess.

This far-reaching development of the apartheid policy had serious implications for the United Party, whose policy of "white leadership with justice" could not stand up to analysis of what it would lead to in the long term. Some members accepted a common voters roll as the future. The majority, prominent among them Douglas Mitchell from Natal, were strongly opposed to it. The issue came to a head at the national congress of the party in Bloemfontein in July 1959, when a resolution by Dr Steenkamp that political representation for the African people in the future must be on the basis of separate rolls, not a common roll, was adopted by a large majority. It was followed by an even more controversial resolution proposed by Douglas Mitchell that the United Party would no longer support the purchase of land which had been promised to be added to the native reserves in 1936, on the ground that in terms of the government's policy such land could now become part of independent Bantu homelands. This resolution was also passed by more than two thirds of the delegates. In the eyes of the minority it constituted a breach of the promise given to Africans in the "settlement" of 1936.

The adoption of these resolutions led to twelve members of parliament resigning from the United Party and forming the Progressive Party, under the leadership of Dr Jan Steytler. The twelve included Helen Suzman, Harry Lawrence, who had been a Minister in General Smuts' government, Zach de Beer, Colin Eglin and Ray Swart. We were soon joined by Walter Stanford, one of the three Native Representatives. I had great difficulty in deserting Sir de Villiers Graaff, leader of the United Party, with whom I had personal connections, and dithered forward and back before deciding that it would be impossible to stay in the United Party while sharing the philosophy of the Progressives.

One of my difficulties in making this move was the question whether I could do so without resigning from parliament. Not only had we been elected on a United Party platform but in my case, when I had been nominated by the United Party I had been required to sign a nomination form which included an undertaking that if I resigned from the party I would resign my seat in parliament. Some Transvaal MPs had done the same, though not those in other parts of the Cape Province: Steytler, Lawrence, de Beer and Eglin, nor those in Natal: Ray Swart, Ronald Butcher and Owen Townley Williams.

To justify not resigning our seats we argued that the United Party at its congress in Bloemfontein had gone back on the solemn undertaking given by a United Party government to black South Africans in 1936 that while taking away certain voting rights it would purchase further land for the native reserves, and that the change in policy at the congress released us from any obligation to resign. We reasoned further that it was urgently necessary for South Africans to get a lead in a new direction away from racially- based policies and that that need overrode our personal obligations. It would have been a killing blow for this initiative if it had had to be put before voters at early by-elections, before it had even been properly formulated. If any of us resigned our seats it would put the others in a poor light. So we decided not to resign and had to ride out the criticism which followed.

The Progressive Party's parliamentary team, January 1960.
Front row: Walter Stanford, Harry Lawrence, Boris Wilson, Jan Steytler,
Helen Suzman, Colin Eglin, Owen Williams.
Back row: Ray Swart, CvR, John Cope, Zach de Beer, Ronald Butcher.

The Progressive Party was officially launched at a congress of 200 delegates in Johannesburg in November of that year, 1959. Its fundamental principle was the rejection of racial discrimination. A committee of experts was to be appointed to make recommendations on constitutional and franchise matters. This committee was appointed early in 1960, chaired by Donald Molteno QC and consisting of talented people. It reported back in 1962, having formulated a comprehensive model for a non-racial and democratic South Africa. The model it recommended was very largely the model which was accepted by the leaders of all sections of the country's peoples at the Codesa negotiations three decades later.

In February 1960, to mark the 50th anniversary of the Union of South Africa, Harold Macmillan, Prime Minister of the United Kingdom, visited South Africa and made his 'wind of change' speech to the members of both Houses of Parliament. It was thought that much of it was written by Sir John Maud, the British High Commissioner in South Africa but the official biography of Mr Macmillan by Alistair Horne records that others had a hand in it, including Lord Home, Julian Amery, Sir Norman Brook, the Cabinet Secretary, and David Hunt of the Commonwealth Office, who accompanied Mr Macmillan on the tour. Mr Macmillan had complimentary things to say about South Africa and the friendship he had received on his visit but also set out plainly the attitude of the British Government to the problem of different races living in the same country, quoting from the statement which had been made by the Foreign Secretary at the United Nations the previous year:

> "In those territories where different races or tribes live side by side, the task is to ensure that all the people may enjoy security and freedom and the chance to contribute as individuals to the progress and well-being of these countries. We reject the idea of any inherent superiority of one race over another. Our policy, therefore, is non-racial; it offers a future in which Africans, Europeans, Asians, the peoples of the Pacific and others with whom we are concerned, will all play their full part as citizens in the countries where they live, and in which feelings of race will be submerged in loyalty to new nations".

Dr Verwoerd in reply thanked him for visiting South Africa and said that while we shared the same ideals we did not necessarily agree on the method of achieving them.

Many years later, in 1983, when the 80th anniversary of the Rhodes Scholarships was celebrated with a reunion of Rhodes Scholars in Oxford, Mr Macmillan as Chancellor of the University spoke at a gala dinner in the garden of Trinity College and I had the opportunity of having a short conversation with him, during which I told him that I had been present to hear his famous speech.

Also in 1960 the republican issue was brought to a head with a referendum of white voters which produced a 52% majority in favour of a republic and led to the proclamation of the Republic of South Africa on 31 May 1961. After the referendum but before the Republic was proclaimed, Dr Verwoerd attended a conference of Commonwealth

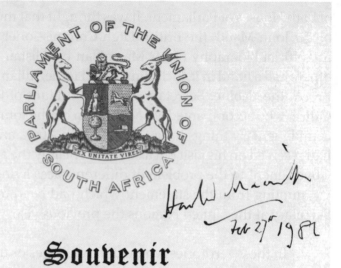

Souvenir

of visit of

The Rt. Hon. HAROLD MACMILLAN
PRIME MINISTER OF THE UNITED KINGDOM

to the

HOUSES OF PARLIAMENT, CAPE TOWN,

on

WEDNESDAY, 3rd FEBRUARY, 1960.

CONTENTS

(1.) Welcome by the Hon. J. H. Conradie, Q.C., Speaker of the House of Assembly.

(2.) Address by the Rt. Hon. Harold Macmillan to Members of both Houses of Parliament in the Parliamentary Dining Room.

(3.) Vote of thanks by Dr. the Hon. H. F. Verwoerd, Prime Minister of the Union of South Africa.

Printed on the Authority of Mr. Speaker.

Cover of the souvenir brochure of Mr Macmillan's visit, later signed by him.

Mr Macmillan making his Wind of Change speech to members of both Houses of
Parliament, 3rd February, 1961. To the right of Mr Macmillan are JH Conradie,
Speaker of the House of Assembly, Dr Verwoerd and Sir de Villiers Graaff.

heads of government in London and although he initially requested
that South Africa be allowed to retain its Commonwealth membership
in spite of becoming a republic, he withdrew this request before the
conference ended. South Africa then left the Commonwealth, a sad
day for many of us.

In the same year, the African National Congress (ANC) and the Pan
Africanist Congress (PAC) launched protests against the pass laws and
after riots in Cape Town and the awful shooting of 69 protesters at
Sharpeville, a State of Emergency was proclaimed which lasted for
some months. The Unlawful Organisations Bill was introduced em-
powering the government to ban political organisations such as the
ANC and PAC. While this was still being debated in parliament there
were reports of a large column of Africans on the road to Cape Town,
headed for the city, possibly for parliament itself. They were led by a
young member of the PAC, Philip Kgosana. The atmosphere in parliament was tense as we saw and heard troops taking up their positions in
front of the building, their rifles clattering on the tar. Kgosana left most

contact

SOUTH AFRICA'S NON-RACIAL FORTNIGHTLY

Registered at G.P.O. as a Newspaper   Every Fortnight 6d.

FORTNIGHT ENDING 16th APRIL 1960   Vol. 3 No. 8

P.A.C. CAMPAIGN REVEALS THE POWER OF NON-VIOLENCE

The Power of Non-Violence: Part of the peaceful crowd of 30,000 people who collected in Cape Town on 30th March, as part of the campaign of the Pan-Africanist Congress.

146

of his estimated 20 000 followers sitting on the side of de Waal Drive just outside the central city while he took about 2000 with him to the main Police Station in Caledon Square. There he asked the senior police officer, Colonel Terblanche, to arrange for him to see the Minister of Justice. The street in front of the police station was tightly packed and the situation was dangerous. With commendable judgment Colonel Terblanche agreed to seek an interview for him with the Minister on condition that he took his followers back to the townships, which he did. Disgracefully, the Minister declined to see Kgosana, though he was prepared to receive a delegation, and within 24 hours Kgosana was taken into custody.

In 1961 Dr Verwoerd called an election early, two years before it was necessary, allegedly with the object of eliminating the Progressives from parliament. This was largely but not fully accomplished as Helen Suzman survived. She won a narrow but famous victory in Houghton and remained in parliament until she retired in 1989,performing an invaluable role in attacking Nationalist policies and actions and working tirelessly to help people who suffered from them. For 13 years she was the sole representative of the Progressive Party but in 1974 five other seats were won by the party. Colin Eglin won in Sea Point and Frederik van Zyl Slabbert in Rondebosch. The Progressives later overtook the United Party as the official opposition.

As a junior MP, first in the United Party and then in the Progressive Party, I concentrated on analysing the bills which were introduced, facilitated by having a legal background, and from time to time speaking on them at the committee stage, when the detail was under consideration. I did not often take part in the main "second reading" debates, though I did so on bills to extend the Group Areas Act. The legislation on which I did the most work was the Promotion of Bantu Self-Government Bill. Our main speakers opposed it on major grounds of principle but there was also room for someone to investigate the geography of the proposed homelands which the government said "could develop to independence". The scattered nature of the areas which had been reserved for Africans made consolidation impracticable. I was given two successive periods of ten minutes at the committee stage of the bill to develop my argument.

17

Back to the Bar, and the Paarl Riot

While in parliament I had taken an office in East London, not quite in my constituency but close to it, and tried to keep something of a legal practice going during the out of session periods. When I lost my seat in 1961 we were pleased to get back permanently into our house in Cape Town and I resumed my practice at the Cape Bar. With two children and another on the way it was not an easy period financially. To have been a politician, let alone one of the Progressive politicians who had "split the opposition" to the Nationalists, was not a qualification to encourage briefs. Cape Town was United Party territory.

In 1962 I was asked to take a brief one would have preferred not to get. There was a serious riot in Paarl, in which over a hundred Africans from the township marched into the town and attacked the police station. They were apparently attempting to free seven men who had been arrested in connection with the murders of other Africans. Thwarted at the police station by gunfire some went on to the prison while others ran riot in the town, burning shops and attacking private houses. A young woman who tried to escape from one of these houses and a man who tried to rescue her were murdered and three other white citizens were badly injured. More shots were fired when a group of about fifty of the rioters attacked policemen trying to get the situation under control. It was stated that five Africans were killed and four others admitted to hospital with bullet wounds. Hundreds of arrests were made and a large number of pangas and metal bars confiscated.

More than a hundred people were charged with the attacks in two big trials. For one of these I and another advocate, Clive Rogers, were asked to defend five accused, including the alleged leaders of the march, and two other advocates, Jimmy Gibson and Gordon Hartford, were asked to defend some twenty others. We were appointed in terms of the rule that when anyone was charged with a crime for which the death sentence was a possibility the Court or the Attorney-General would arrange legal defence on a Pro Deo basis unless the accused chose to brief their own counsel. Pro Deo work was not for no pay at all but the rate of pay was low.

In preparing for the case we were not given as much background information by the people we were defending as came out later when a Supreme Court judge was appointed as a one-man Commission of Inquiry. He then heard evidence presented by counsel on behalf of the Institute of Race Relations that the organisation called Poqo had been building its membership aggressively in the Paarl township of Mbekweni and the nearby shanty town Langabuya and that the murders of Africans which had taken place were connected with this. Poqo had been started by militant members of the Pan Africanist Congress after the latter organisation was banned in 1960. In Mbekweni there were 20 families and more than 2000 "single" men, many of them married but unable to bring their wives from the Transkei to the Western Cape because of influx control regulations. The Western Cape was at that time a coloured preference area and the permits required by African work-seekers to be in the area were not readily given. Witnesses alleged corruption on the part of the Municipal Director of African Affairs and the senior African clerk in the issuing of such permits. They reported rough handling and regular raiding of the barracks at night by the municipal police to check on illegal entrants and rent defaulters. They said there was no adequate avenue for expression of grievances. The situation gave rise to intense frustration and was fertile ground for insurrection.

Of the five accused whom Rogers and I represented, two had decided not to give evidence and declined to brief us with their story. I think they did not want to recognise the court and its trial. They were firm in their attitude, without appearing antagonistic to us. As the trial progressed a number of witnesses called by the prosecution identified them as having led the march and it became clear that our effort on their behalf had to be directed at distancing them from the attacks on the people killed or injured. That seemed our best hope of saving them from the death sentence. This also became our main object in defending the third accused, Felix Jaxa. He was happy to accept our services and to work with us but the state witnesses also described him as one of the leaders of the march, to an extent which became difficult to refute. Our other two accused claimed they had not been in the march or the attacks, making our mandate for them straightforward.

The trial went on for many weeks, lengthened by trials within the main trial to test whether incriminating statements which had been made by a number of accused (not ours) to the police should be ruled inadmissible because of undue pressure put on them by the police. During this time Rogers and I saw our accused quite a few times and found Felix Jaxa an intelligent and likeable human being.

The state's evidence of the march on the police station identified most of the accused as having been on the march but they did not manage to identify anyone as having personally attacked the people who had been killed or injured. There was insufficient reliable evidence against the two of our five accused who claimed that they had not been on the march and they were acquitted. Sadly our other three were found guilty of the serious charges and were sentenced to death. Apart from murder I do not remember the precise charges which were brought against them but factually they were found guilty of having led the column of marchers into the town to attack the police station, some of whom had gone into private homes and attacked inhabitants, killing two and wounding others. The other accused who were found guilty of having marched on the police station, but not as leaders, were given periods of imprisonment.

It was a distressing result and Clive Rogers and I felt particularly distressed about Felix Jaxa. There were no grounds for a successful appeal to the Appellate Division.

Two or three months later I received a telephone call from Pretoria Central Prison, and Jaxa was put on the line. He had asked to be allowed to phone to thank Rogers and me for our efforts on behalf of him and the other two. Later I also received a letter from him, written the day before they were hanged. It speaks for itself.

That such a person could be driven to violence and be hanged for it was an awful indictment of the system.

Felix F. Jaxa No V. 475
Central Prison
Box 410
Pretoria
31st October, 1968.

Mr. Advocate C.B. Van Ryneveld.
No 1 Dorp Street,
Cape Town.

Dear Sir,

I write this letter to express my gratitude to you. Actually we are all very grateful for the defence you did in order to save our souls. That you have failed to defend us so that at least we should get years imprisonment, must not discourage you.

I heard what you said in the telephone and I think perhaps God will accept our souls because we leave the flesh on earth. With an open heart I wish God may bless you all. I shall never forget your courtesy in your defence. I believe you did all what you could do for us; we cannot blame you just because we are now going to the gallows.

At the moment we are still happy though tomorrow we are leaving this earth of sin and woe. We think that God will forgive us our sins because we have prayed and you too have wished us a good way to Him. And we in turn wish you Sir, a happy life while you are still on earth. There is another world which I say you must pray whole-heartedly for it because the path is wide which goes to hell and many take it, but the path is narrow which goes to everlasting life and very few will take it.

I do not say I am a righteous man and that I will go to the kingdom of God but I have tried my best. But God does not come and say to a man "Your sins are forgiven".

Pass my regards to advocates Rogers Gibson and Mr. Hartford.

I beg to remain.
Yours faithfully,
Felix F. Jaxa.

Letter from Felix Jaxa, one of the three leaders
of the Paarl riot, from Central Prison, Pretoria.

151

18

A More Rewarding Brief

*I*n 1966 I was briefed as a junior, initially to Philip Schock, QC, later to Graeme Duncan, QC, in the case of *Bader and Another* v *Weston and Another.* Our client was the First Respondent, Garfield Weston. He was reputed to be the world's biggest baker and grocer. Even I knew of Weston Biscuits. He had visited South Africa on holiday more than once and had bought a house in Constantia. He became interested in extending his milling activities to South Africa and on behalf of Associated British Foods in England, of which he was Chairman and the controlling shareholder, he acquired a controlling interest in the leading milling company in South Africa, Premier Milling.

Before that the controlling interest in Premier Milling had been held by a company of which Gerald Jaffee was a substantial shareholder. Jaffee was a director of Premier Milling and he remained a director after Weston acquired control for Associated British Foods.

The association of Weston and Jaffee in Premier Milling led to a joint venture. Jaffee was invited to bring to Weston's attention suitable industrial companies which might be acquired. One such company which he introduced was Bailes, a manufacturer of twines and bags for the sugar industry. Jaffee suggested that this should be acquired through another company, Grainbag International, which purchased and reconditioned grain bags. The main shareholder in the latter was Leslie Bader, who was related to Jaffee. As Premier Milling was the largest user of cotton bags in South Africa there was logic in the suggested acquisitions.

It was decided to acquire them and to form a private company in which to hold them. This was formed and named Bagmeni Holdings Limited. The two acquisitions were paid for by loan finance from Weston. Weston took 70% of Bagmeni's shares, the other 30% going to Jaffee, Bader, Laurie Jaffee and Regsel (Pty) Ltd., a Jaffee and Bader company. Bader was appointed managing director of Bailes and he also continued to run the company he had run before, Grainbag International. Other companies were acquired: Entumeni Sugar Milling and its property company Entumeni Estates; and SA Litho, all with the help of loan finance from Weston.

Unfortunately Weston soon became disenchanted with Bader and wanted to terminate his association with him in Bagmeni. He had the board of directors reconstituted and became chairman and a director himself and Bader was asked to resign his directorships in the group. Among other measures Weston gave notice that he required the repayment of part of his loan to Bagmeni and proposed the sale of SA Litho to enable this to be done. This and other actions brought him into conflict with Jaffee as well as Bader and resulted in the court proceedings against him. Bader and Jaffee alleged in their application that he was acting in a manner which was unfair and oppressive to them as minority shareholders of Bagmeni and sought an order that he buy out their shares in Bagmeni at a value to be put on them by the Court.

Such a case was right up the street of Philip Schock, who was briefed on behalf of Weston. The brief came from a prominent firm of solicitors in Johannesburg, Hayman, Godfrey& Sanderson, through an equally prominent firm in Cape Town, Syfret, Godlonton & Low. Philip was a highly intelligent and shrewd advocate, with an appearance a little like Shylock, though more pleasant. He analysed the allegations in the petition and the requirements of the section of the Companies Act on which it was based with great thoroughness, over and over. Our preparations were invariably interrupted in mid-morning by a telephone call from his stockbroker, because he was an avid investor in the stock market.

In our initial short appearance in court he asked for and was granted an adjournment of two months to enable opposing affidavits to be drawn up in the matter, considering its complicated nature and the fact that Weston was in England. In working on these he decided to take a preliminary objection which looked to have merit as a first reply, without answering the main allegations in the petition. He disguised the point in a general statement that the petition failed to make out a case for the relief sought, in order to avoid warning the applicants and giving them the chance to remedy the defect by giving notice of an amendment before the hearing. Further, although he would have argued the point as well as anyone, he decided that it was better presented by Graeme Duncan, the leading and most respected senior advocate at the Cape Bar. Because the point did not go to the heart of the matter there was a risk that it might not have been well received. Two other less promising preliminary objections were included in the reply.

Weston's shares in Bagmeni were held in a company and Weston and the company were both cited as Respondents. Graeme Duncan represented Weston, with me as junior, and Philip Schock represented the company, with Gerald Friedman as his junior. Harry Snitcher, QC, appeared for Bader and Sam Aaron, SC, for Gerald Jaffee, briefed by Sonnenberg, Hoffmann & Galombik, another leading firm of solicitors. On the bench was Corbett, J, later to become Chief Justice and in that capacity to officiate at the inauguration of Nelson Mandela as President in 1994. It was quite a gathering of Cape Town's senior lawyers.

Schock's tactics went according to plan. The main preliminary point was upheld, though Mick Corbett was critical of Respondents' failure to file their main opposing affidavits at the same time as taking the preliminary point and made the Petitioners pay only two-thirds of Respondents' costs. In spite of that it was a very satisfactory first blow.

Leave was given to the Petitioners to remedy the defect in their petition; Respondents were given 4 weeks to file their opposing affidavits; and Petitioners were given 3 weeks after that to file their replying affidavits.

As there were disputes of fact the matter could not be resolved without oral evidence. Graeme Duncan had been ideal for the legal argument at the first hearing but Philip now recommended that for the trial the services of a Transvaal QC, Gert Coetsee, QC, should be obtained, as he was regarded as the best cross-examiner in South Africa.

The Petitioners' first witness was an accountant, Harold Gorvy, called to put a generous value on the Petitioners' shares in Bagmeni, which they were applying for Weston to be ordered to purchase. This gave scope for a protracted cross-examination, because Bagmeni had more than a dozen subsidiary companies, each of which had to be valued. Gert Coetsee had worked up an intimate knowledge of the balance sheets. The valuation of the Petitioners' minority shareholdings in the holding company Bagmeni gave further great scope for challenge, because minority stakes in private companies are notoriously difficult to value and in this case there was the added factor that Bagmeni's finances were largely dependent on Weston's goodwill. Harold Gorvy had been three days in the witness-box without getting near the end of Coetsee's cross-examination when an approach came to settle the whole matter. Bader and Jaffee got modest amounts for their shares and Bader took his grainbag company back as part of his consideration.

Within six months I was to leave the Bar to join Hill Samuel Merchant Bank SA, the South African subsidiary of the English bank of the same name. I left the bar with regret, because there was a camaraderie among the advocates of the Cape Bar which added a lot to the enjoyment of one's working life.

19

John Passmore and the John Passmore Trust

Although the achievements of John Passmore in developing facilities for African cricket in Cape Town and a tournament Week for African schoolchildren nationally during the apartheid years were perhaps not major in the 140 year history of African cricket in South Africa described by Andre Odendaal in his handsome book *The Story of an African Game*, they were in their period and context outstanding, resulting in Passmore being called the father (sometimes godfather) of black cricket.

Born in 1911 Passmore grew up in Kimberley but in 1928 went to England and worked for the Diamond Corporation. When war broke out in 1939 he joined the British forces and served in Cairo and Syria before being selected for a special patrol detachment in General Wingate's Chindits. He was more than once parachuted into the Burmese jungle behind Japanese lines. After the war he returned to South Africa and from 1946 to 1987 worked for Premier Wire, a manufacturing company, first as accountant, then as secretary, and finally as financial director.

He was Chairman of the Western Province Cricket Club from 1962 to 1967 and on the executive of the Western Province Cricket Union from 1969 to 1984. In 1970, after John Vorster had refused to accept the MCC team which included D'Oliveira, the South African Cricket

Association made a grant of R50 000 to an SACA Trust "to assist the development of non-white cricket" and asked John to be a trustee, together with Eddie Carter, Chief Executive of Syfrets Trust, and JP Duminy, former principal of the University of Cape Town.

The South African Cricket Association (SACA) was at that stage trying to reach out to the then leading non-white unions, the South African African Cricket Board (SAACB), which catered for most African cricketers, and the South African Cricket Board of Control (SACBOC), the non-racial body which represented mainly coloured and Indian cricketers but also a limited number of Africans. A formal meeting of the three bodies was held in 1972 and an umbrella body, the Cricket Council of South Africa, was formed in which SACA and SAACB agreed to participate but not SACBOC, led by Hassan Howa. The latter wanted a unitary, not a federal body, and mixed cricket at club, provincial and national level.

Four years later, in 1976, renewed unity discussions were held between the three unions aimed at introducing "normal" cricket ie. mixed cricket from club level upwards. Dr Koornhof, the Minister of Sport, had made statements suggesting some relaxation of the prohibition of mixed sport. While the unity talks were going on the announcement of a tour by an International Wanderers team to South Africa, captained by Greg Chappell and managed by Richie Benaud, precipitated a crisis in SACBOC. Under its new President, Rashid Varachia, SACBOC accepted an invitation from SACA to participate in matches against the touring team but the executive of its strongest affiliated body, the Western Province Cricket Board, opposed the decision and some of its members resigned from SACBOC. This opposing faction, led by Howa, took control of the Western Province Cricket Board. They argued that there could be no normal cricket in an abnormal society.

In the following year, 1977, SACBOC and SAACB joined (some said "were swallowed up by") the SACA in a new body named the South African Cricket Union, with Varachia as President, and those who opposed the attempt to introduce "normal" cricket while the apartheid order remained formed the South African Cricket Board, led by Howa. Cricket in South Africa was played under these two bodies until unity was achieved in 1991. The South African Cricket Union favoured playing cricket as best it could be played, ie. "mixed" to the extent allowed; while the South African Cricket Board put political considerations above the playing of cricket. This difference of approach is well described in Mogamad Allie's book on the history of the Western Province Cricket Board from 1959 to 1991, aptly titled *More than a Game*.

Coming back to cricket among Africans, as distinguished from coloureds and Indians: at the time of the 1972 discussions the SA African Cricket Board was prepared to work with the SA Cricket Association (as it was then called) to get better facilities for African cricketers and they suggested that the SACA Trust money be applied to funding an African schools week along the lines of the successful Nuffield Week. This was agreed and the first tournament was planned for Bloemfontein in December 1971, with John Passmore in the driving seat. He discovered that there was no suitable ground for Africans in Bloemfontein and switched the tournament to Cape Town. The week was a success and continued annually in different centres for nineteen years, managed by John. It became known as the Passmore Week. From 1985 a team chosen from each Passmore Week took part in Nuffield Week.

Though the facilities for African cricket in Cape Town were better than in Bloemfontein, they were hopelessly inadequate. The field in Langa, the oldest African township in Cape Town, was a rough piece of ground with virtually no grass. John enlisted the help of an engineering friend and had the field levelled and grassed. He set about raising money through a Western Province African Cricket Trust (Westpact) and before long added nets, a second cricket field and a pavilion. By 1975 the ground was in good shape for a match between a visiting Derrick Robins X1 and a SA African X1, the first time a white side had played in an African township. In the 1980s the complex was formally named the John Passmore Oval in honour of John. Ali Bacher, CEO of the SA Cricket Union, flew down from Johannesburg for the ceremony.

To appreciate John's contribution at Langa one needs to remember that few white people went into black townships during those troubled apartheid years. The Langa riots of 1960, followed by the declaration of a State of Emergency and the banning of the ANC and

John Passmore, right, and Fritz Bing, President of WPCU, at the naming
of the Langa stadium The John Passmore Oval.

PAC, were still alive in people's memories. 1963 was another bad year
in Langa, with three incidents of policemen being killed. John went to
see what facilities for cricket were available and became so well known
and appreciated in Langa that he could go in without apprehension,
even when there were political disturbances. The Langa Cricket Club
grew strong with his help and by the end of the 1980s was fielding
seven junior sides, from under 11 to under 19, and two, sometimes
three, "senior" teams. The latter often included schoolboys and they
played in leagues of the "white" Western Province Cricket Union. In
1988/9 John also developed a field and clubhouse in Nyanga township,
although cricket did not take off there to the same extent. The field was
in fact used more for rugby than for cricket.

John's thinking was set out in a brochure he produced to raise
funds. He wrote:

"If you want to promote racial harmony in South Africa today
there is no better place to start than on the sportsfield.
People of different backgrounds mix more easily and more
naturally in sport than elsewhere.

The provision of sporting facilities is the quickest, least expensive and quite possibly the most successful way of improving the quality of life among less-privileged people."

In early 1990, a year before John died, Nelson Mandela was released and by the middle of 1991 the control of cricket was transformed. The South African Cricket Union and the South African Cricket Board joined forces in a new United Cricket Board, with Ali Bacher and Khaya Majola as joint managing directors. In Cape Town the Western Province Cricket Union and the non-racial Western Province Cricket Board joined forces in a new Western Province Cricket Association, with 50-50 representation on all committees.

Nationally, except in Cape Town, cricket for Africans had gone backwards from 1971 to 1991. Andre Odendaal in his *Story of an African Game* went so far as to say that "cricket in African communities was on its way to extinction by the end of the apartheid era". In the cricket played under the auspices of SACBOC and later SACB, based in coloured and Indian areas, only 9 out of 450 cricketers who played inter-provincial cricket between 1971 and 1991 were Africans. Khaya Majola was notable among them. Odendaal continued: "The only other signs of life were the still-segregated Passmore Schools Cricket Week and the Langa Cricket Club in Cape Town patronised by John Passmore". In the difficult apartheid order that reflected a remarkable achievement by John.

John died in 1991. He had been keen that his work should continue after his death and in 1989 had launched the John Passmore Trust for the purpose, and asked me to be its chairman. Among the trustees, initially, were Morne du Plessis, Judge Jan Steyn, Judge Pat Tebbutt, Neil McCarthy, Benny Rabinowitz and Jeremy Day and later Gerald Njengele, Vincent van der Bijl, Bob Woolmer, David Dewar, Tex van Beuge and Bruce Risien. None of us matched the personal time and effort John had put in but the Trust remained active. In keeping the afternoon sessions going for junior players we used a lively sportswoman, Gill Taylor, to run them and she did a good deal more than that. She was a good hockey player and coached hockey at the stadium in the winter. Hockey had been introduced there by Bob Woolmer.

One afternoon in the 1990s when Brian Johnston was in Cape Town he expressed interest in going to the Langa stadium and I took him there. The nets were in full swing and Brian was very impressed. A young wicket-keeper Thami Tsolikele was practising with his gloves and Brian, who in his playing days had kept wicket, insisted on a picture being taken of the two of them, crouched for action. The young Tsolikele later played for South Africa on tour, and captained Western Province.

We ran the two trusts, Westpact and the John Passmore Trust, together, raising and spending of the order of R100 000 in most years from 1991 to 1997. The John Passmore name and record made it not too difficult to elicit donations, though it was time-consuming. There were some substantial donations among numerous less substantial ones. I remember in particular a donation of R25 000 from my brother Tony and generous donations from the Stanley Lewis Foundation, the Philip Schock Foundation, of which Arnold Galombik was a trustee, and the Norton Ramsay Foundation. A former Transvaler, Pearce Rood, who had settled in London, where he was a partner in an international law firm, formed an English charitable trust, the John Passmore Trust UK, with Peter May as chairman and Brian Johnston as one of the trustees, and we received handsome donations from them, and a big consignment of new and used cricket equipment, which I had some difficulty in clearing from the docks, not least in clearing it without paying duties. Pearce Rood also arranged four annual donations of 5000 pounds each from the Colin Lowndes Trust in Jersey, which inter alia paid for extensions to the pavilion and changing rooms.

We were in regular contact with the new Western Province Cricket Association and they helped us with funding. After unity was achieved in 1991 they had their hands full improving the facilities of the large number of ex-WPCB clubs, including clubs with teams in the Premier League, and were pleased that we were giving special attention to Langa. The Langa first team was promoted two divisions to the division below the Premier League, somewhat misleadingly called the first division.

When two or three years had passed after cricket unity both the WPCA and the John Passmore trustees felt that the WPCA should take full responsibility for assisting cricket in Langa and other African townships. The Trust continued to assist and two events in which the Trust was involved in 1995 and 1997 warrant recording.

The first was the visit of the Queen and the Duke of Edinburgh to a mini-sports festival at the Langa stadium in 1995, hosted by the Trust. It had been preceded by the visit of John Major to South Africa the previous year, accompanied on the sporting side by Colin Cowdrey and Rob Andrew, the England flyhalf. Through the British High Commissioner, Anthony Reeve, Jan Steyn and I invited Mr Major to visit Newlands cricket ground. He could not fit this into his programme but invited us, together with others from the WPCA, the Western Province Cricket Club and the Passmore Trust, to meet him and Colin Cowdrey at the British High Commission offices in Cape Town. He asked about cricket in the townships and we told him about Langa and the Passmore Trust. At a news conference before leaving South Africa he announced that the Lord's Taverners, of which Colin was President, had agreed to donate a Sports Bus to the Passmore Trust.

Shortly before the Queen and the Duke were to come to Cape Town the following year the High Commissioner's office advised us that the Queen wished to visit the Langa Sports Stadium and that during the visit the Duke of Edinburgh, who was the Patron and Twelfth Man of the Taverners, would hand over the keys of the Sports Bus. A festival of mini-sports was arranged – cricket, hockey and rugby – with the onlookers largely restricted to parents of the participants. All went according to plan as the royal party arrived. The Minister of Sport, Steve Tshwete, and township sport officials were presented to the Queen and the Duke and they were taken first towards the mini-cricket, then in full swing. As we came closer a ball (soft) was hit unexpectedly hard nearly in our direction, with a young fielder in hot pursuit. I could see that the ball was going past us a good few yards away but the Queen was not so certain and put her arms out as if to catch or stop it. A photographer from *Die Burger* managed to catch the moment and his sequence of two photographs made the front page of *Die Burger* the next day. The High Commissioner described them as the photographic scoop of the Queen's tour!

After a short viewing of the mini-cricket we walked over to where the Sports Bus was to be presented. Before we could get there young sportsmen from the many games being played abandoned their games for a closer view of the Queen and the Duke and at the same time a crowd of more than a hundred local residents who had collected outside the entrance to the stadium forced their way past the police, claiming that it was their community stadium, and came towards the Queen and the Duke in an enthusiastic rush. The ribbon tapes intended to keep onlookers at a reasonable distance from the handing-over ceremony had no chance against the new spectators and the Queen and Duke were surrounded in the crowd. It was quickly decided to abort the ceremony. The Duke made his way to me and put the keys of the Sports Bus into my hands; the Queen's bodyguards ushered her and the Duke back to their Range Rover; and off they went. The Queen appeared to take the occasion in her stride, saying

How's that! Her Majesty The Queen with Clive van Ryneveld and a speedy fielder

LANGA TOWNSHIP, outside Cape Town
March 21: Her Majesty The Queen and His
Royal Highness The Duke of Edinburgh
presented the keys of a Lord's Taverners'
New Horizons minibus to Clive van
Ryneveld, chairman of the John Passmore
Trust.

Elizabeth R

**Escorting the Queen at the John Passmore Oval, Langa, 1995.
The Queen sensed a potential collision with a mini-cricketer.**

afterwards that she had had similar experiences in Africa before and that she and the Duke had been unworried but we were not proud of our preparations.

The Sports Bus, with sign-writing brightly displaying its origins and credentials, had its home at the headquarters of the WPCA in Newlands and for two years rendered valuable service for the Passmore Trust and for the WPCA in transporting in particular young black cricketers. Sadly it was then stolen and not recovered. Gert Bam, a development officer of the WPCA, took it to the airport to fetch a visiting team and while he waited in the terminal building for the team to arrive the sports bus disappeared from the parking area. We were able to buy another bus with the insurance money, topped up, but it was a sad loss.

There was a sequel to *Die Burger's* photographer catching the mini-cricketer and the Queen in action. Her personal assistant, Lord Robert Fellowes, also appeared in the background of the two photographs. Fourteen years later in 2009 he was in Cape Town as a trustee

Langa 1995. It was optimistic to think the crowd would stay behind the tapes.

of the Rhodes Trust for a Rhodes Scholars function (held in ex-President Nelson Mandela's private house in Constantia) and in conversation he recalled the incident at Langa and asked whether I would like him to ask the Queen to sign the pair of photographs. I said I would indeed. I struggled to get a good copy of the photographs. *Die Burger* could not trace either the photographs or the photographer. In the end I had a laser copy made of the page on which the photographs appeared in the magazine of the Lord's Taverners and sent it to Lord Fellowes. Before long it was returned with the Royal signature and a report of the Queen's comment when signing it: "There's Robert in the outfield again". It was an apt comment because Lord Fellowes has been for some years a member of the committee of the MCC and a keen follower of cricket.

The other special Trust event of that period was the tour of an under 15 team from Cape Town's black townships to England in 1997. The idea came from Sir John (or Ian) Maclure, headmaster of Croftinloan School at Pitlochry in Scotland, whom I had met at Langa while he was in Cape Town on holiday with his South African-born wife, Jane. I was paying a casual visit to the Langa stadium and found John (who introduced himself to me as Ian) doing the same. He had heard of the cricket at Langa and out of interest had gone to have a look. In 1996, on his next holiday visit, he spent some time coaching the Langa under 14 team. Back in England he sent an invitation to the Passmore Trust to send an under 15 team from the black townships to play against school teams in Devon and Cornwall, offering to arrange the accommodation and hopefully to raise the funds for the airfares.

This was an attractive invitation but the funding seemed a tall order. We certainly couldn't expect Ian to find it all in England. In Cape Town our case for asking for donations for a tour like this was much weaker since the Trust was no longer the main player in assisting African cricket in Cape Town. We were bold enough to say to Ian: yes, subject to success in raising the money, but for some months our fundraising in England and Cape Town was not sufficient to go ahead. Then I heard that Jim Sutcliffe, who held a senior position in Prudential Assurance, UK, had worked for Southern Life in Newlands, and was interested in cricket. I faxed him a request for assistance and in quick time the Prudential promised 5000 pounds. That covered virtually the whole gap between what we had raised and what we needed.

In June 1997 thirteen young black cricketers from Langa and other Cape Town townships flew to Heathrow for a tour of nine matches against schools and other young teams in Devon and Cornwall. Teams from well-known schools such as Winchester, Oundle and Blundell's were included. Ezra Cagwe, a member of the WPCA staff, went with them as coach, and Fezile Mguqulwa, chairman of primary schools cricket in the townships, went as their manager. Needless to say, Ian organised everything delightfully at the UK end, except the weather. His wife Jane drove the minibus which transported the team most of the way. The weather interfered seriously with the cricket and the team did not have great success in the matches they played but it was a tremendous experience for them.

Although its role in promoting black cricket in the Western Cape has diminished the Passmore Trust, with first Tex van Beuge and then Bruce Risien as chairman, has continued to assist black cricketers.

In the course of visits to Langa I got to know two leading Langa personalities, Gerald Njengele and Solomon Makosana. Opportunities for people living in mainly white residential areas to meet and make friendships with people from the black townships were few.

Gerald Njengele was already headmaster of Zimasa, one of the big schools in Langa, when I met him in the early 1990s. Like almost all schools in the black townships they had no sportsfield and the boys who were keen to play cricket played at the Langa Cricket Club. Zimasa had very poor classrooms and the headmaster's office from which Gerald ran the school was a totally inadequate tiny room. He successfully raised money from the Douglas Murray Trust and other sources for a new school on alternative land. Its buildings are chalk and cheese from the old ones. He is still headmaster of Zimasa today.

He is also President of Guguletu Cricket Club, which has 3 senior teams and 5 junior teams but only one field. As a result many of their games have to be played away and the cost of transport (R400 per match for a minibus) is a big burden. In 2011 "Passmore" friend Pearce Rood, living in England, has donated R10 000 to help with transport and coaching.

Solomon Makosana obtained degrees in history at the University of Cape Town and in education at the University of the Western Cape and taught at schools in Langa and Guguletu before being appointed principal of Nomlinganiselo Primary School in Nyanga. In his playing days he was an opening batsman and medium-paced bowler and played for Langa Cricket Club. He obtained a coaching diploma and coached at Langa Cricket Club while John Passmore was involved there.

He was elected Deputy President of the Western Province Cricket Association in 2005 and took over as President later in the year. Sadly he died in 2006.

After retiring as principal of his school he became Chief Executive Officer of the Amy Biehl Foundation in 2001. The story of this foundation is a sad but also special one. Amy Biehl was an American girl who was involved in an anti-apartheid campaign while a student at Stanford University. As a Fulbright scholar she came to the University of the Western Cape and worked with its Community Law Centre on issues of women's rights. She was moved by the poverty she saw in the black townships and made friends with students from Guguletu. In driving them home one night in 1993 she was attacked and killed by youths in the township, the very people she was doing much to help. Her parents showed no bitterness but gave money to set up the foundation to further Amy's ideals.

Solomon had a good sense of humour. While he was President of the Western Province Cricket Association I was asked to give a talk (the annual New Year lecture which Andre Odendaal has organised) on the changes in our cricket since the time I played and Solomon asked me for a cv so that he could introduce me. I made the most of my CV and sent it to him. In his introduction he brandished the CV and said, "In the townships, Clive, with a CV like this, we could make your funeral go on all day!" Funerals are big events in the African community. Many Africans take out insurance to cover the cost. During the apartheid years, when meetings were often banned, funerals were usually exempted and were often used for political speeches.

20

South Africa's Cricket Isolation

A sad aspect of our cricket isolation was that it came when we had our strongest ever side which could have taken us to the top of international cricket. In his book *Fingleton on Cricket*, published in 1972, Jack Fingleton wrote:

> "The present South African team is the best in the country's history. It is, to my mind, undoubtedly the best side in the world today. … I doubt whether an international team of any era possessed at one time two such devastating batsmen as Graeme Pollock and Barry Richards. One day in 1970 in Durban, they tore the Australian attack apart, the South Africans declaring with the phenomenal score of 9-622 an hour after lunch on the second day! Australia, in this series, suffered its heaviest defeat in Test history, 4-nil."

In his chapter on left hand batsmen in the same book Fingleton described Graeme Pollock's two centuries at Sydney and Adelaide in the 1963/4 tour in glowing terms. After the former he said Pollock retired to an acclaim seldom heard on a cricket field. After the latter he said Gary Sobers was one of the spectators who rose to their feet to applaud Pollock back.

Barry Richards received high praise from none less than Don Bradman. The latter wrote a foreword for Barry's book *Barry Richards on Cricket* in which he said:

> "I venture the opinion that no player has ever come to
> Australia and given us more superb exhibitions of batting.
> There were the usual hallmarks of greatness – plenty of time
> to play his shots, calm and correct footwork, beautiful timing,
> splendid placing of the ball and a complete range of shots."

Apart from Pollock and Richards we had outstanding all-rounders in Barlow, Proctor (batsman/bowler) and Lindsay (wicket-keeper/batsman), as well as Bacher, who had made 12 first-class centuries in addition to captaining the team.

I wonder whether the cricket boycott might possibly not have developed if the South African Cricket Association had dissociated itself strongly from the government's decision to refuse the MCC side which included D'Oliveira. I attended the first annual general meeting of the SACA after the cancellation of the tour as a Western Province representative and argued for a statement by the association to that effect. Unfortunately I didn't do it very well, first raising the issue under the wrong agenda item, and as a newcomer to SACA meetings and known to have been a politician, my proposal didn't carry much weight. Jack Cheetham was President and he was not persuaded.

Two years later, in 1970, when the next tour by South Africa to England was due but was running into opposition in England, Jack did make a statement on behalf of the SACA that future South African teams touring overseas would be chosen on merit but by then the protest movement had gathered momentum to the extent that the British government asked the Cricket Council to withdraw its invitation to tour. The next scheduled tour to Australia in 1971/2 was also cancelled.

I was keen to see the end of apartheid but did not want South Africa out of international cricket and did not agree with the boycott. Its target was the South African government but the government and most of its supporters had little interest in cricket. The people most hurt by the boycott were the cricketers, of whom a large majority were opposed to the government's apartheid policy.

A prominent figure campaigning for the isolation of South African cricket was David Sheppard, fine international batsman who became the Bishop of Liverpool. I had finished at Oxford just before he played for Cambridge but I played against him when touring England in 1951 with Dudley Nourse's team. In 1989 David came to South Africa to see the situation on the spot. In Johannesburg Ali Bacher took him to Tembisa, a black township (where he said he noted only 3 sports-grounds serving 45 schools), and in Cape Town John Passmore and I met him in a small mixed gathering. The discussion was more on apart-heid generally than on how our cricket was progressing. When he got back he wrote an article for *The Cricketer* entitled "Little for your Com-fort", imitating the title of Bishop Trevor Huddleston's book *Naught for your Comfort*. The punch-line was: "It is unthinkable to me that there should be any relaxing of sporting, political, or economic pressures at this critical moment". John Passmore replied in the January 1990 edi-tion of *The Cricketer* pleading for sporting pressures to be left out of it but David wrote back to John reiterating the need to keep up pressure, including sporting pressure, if peaceful change was to come about. He accepted that it would mean that some developments would be lim-ited now for the good of another generation.

By then the government's prohibition of mixed sport had been con-siderably relaxed and my view was that the emphasis should have been on taking advantage of the relaxations. Fortunately Nelson Mandela was released from detention the following year and the whole picture changed.

I accept that South Africa's cricket isolation was part of a wider cam-paign of isolation, particularly economic, which together with the armed struggle played a big part in persuading the government to do a u-turn.

I heard a cheerful anecdote of David Sheppard and Freddie Trueman, possibly apocryphal. David had retired from big cricket to go into the church but heeded a plea by the English selectors to join the MCC team to tour Australia in 1962. Fielding in the slips he dropped a catch off Trueman's bowling, earning a frustrated reaction from Freddie: "I don't mind you shutting your eyes when you pray, vicar, but for heaven's sake keep them open when I'm bowling".

Ali Bacher, as managing director of the South African Cricket Union, worked hard at getting South Africa back into the fold and also at pro-moting black cricket, particularly through his Cricket Development Programme for the youth of Soweto, Atteridgeville and Alexandra.

In 1988 he organised a great celebration in Johannesburg and Port Elizabeth to mark the 100th anniversary of South Africa in test cricket and invited leading international cricketers from England, Australia and New Zealand, the countries we had played against. Between 30 and 40 international players from overseas came, including 12 captains. I was delighted to renew contact with cricketers such as Peter May, Ian Craig, George Mann, Walter Hadlee, Merv Wallace, Lindsay Hassett, John Reid, Bert Sutcliffe, Neil Harvey, Freddie Trueman and Trevor Bailey, all of whom I had played against. There were others I hadn't played against but was delighted to meet – Bob Wyatt, Keith Miller, Mike Smith, Tony Lewis and Geoff Boycott. The two major events of the celebration were two big banquets for over 1000 guests each in Alberton, near Johannesburg, and in the big hall of the University of Port Elizabeth.

It was heartening to see that although we were not yet back in test cricket, we retained the friendship and goodwill of these international cricketers.

International cricketers at the 1988 celebration of South Africa's 100 years in test cricket.
Row 1: van der Merwe, Smith, Harvey, Hughes, Craig, Bacher, Fletcher, Boycott
Row 2: Lewis, McGlew, Reid, CvR.
Row 3: Edrich, Johnson, Hadlee, Hassett, Wyatt, Wallace, May, Mann.
Row 4: Rice, Sutcliffe, Kirsten, Procter.

21

Two Rhodes Scholar Reunions

*T*here have been two big reunion gatherings of Rhodes scholars, one in 1983, to celebrate the 80th anniversary of the scholarships, and the other in their centenary year, 2003.

It is impressive that the scholarship scheme which Cecil John Rhodes created in his will more than a hundred years ago has enabled 7000 students to study at Oxford and is still going strong.

The garden front of Rhodes House, Oxford.

In his will Rhodes directed his trustees to establish 52 scholarships at Oxford annually, twenty of them for countries forming part of the British Empire, described as Colonial Scholarships, and thirty-two for the United States. Of the Colonial Scholarships three were for Rhodesia and five for South Africa, including one for each of four schools: Diocesan College, Rondebosch; St Andrews College, Grahamstown; Paul Roos, Stellenbosch and the South African College School, Cape Town.

In a codicil to the will Rhodes added five annual German scholarships. During the two Great Wars the German scholarships were suspended or cancelled and they were only reinstated in part some years after. South Africa benefited from the cancellation of the German scholarships during the 1914-18 war, for three new scholarships were given to South Africa: one to the Transvaal; one to the Orange Free State and one to alternate between Port Elizabeth and Kimberley, where Rhodes had established the De Beers mining company in 1880. In 1922 a further scholarship was given to the Cape Province.

Today there are still nine South African scholarships but the five provincial scholarships have been converted into "South Africa-at-large" scholarships, competed for on a national basis. The school scholarships remain as directed in Rhodes' will – but they have had to survive two attacks on them during the apartheid years on the ground that they were available to white students only and therefore, so it was argued, conflicted with clause 24 of the will, which provided that "no student shall be qualified or disqualified for election to a scholarship on account of his race or religious opinions".

The first attack commenced in 1970, led by two African/American Rhodes scholars. They circulated a petition among the Rhodes scholars in residence, stating that the South African and Rhodesian scholarships should be discontinued unless a fair number of black Rhodes scholars were elected in the two countries. Of the 145 scholars in residence 85 signed the petition, including a few South Africans. The petition was considered by the trustees and they resolved ("with reluctance") to take legal steps to broaden the basis of eligibility for the South African scholarships. In particular they planned to have the four school scholarships converted to South Africa-at-Large scholarships.

Not surprisingly the four schools rallied to protect their scholarships. A committee was formed and I was asked to chair it. Tony

173

Mallett, headmaster of Diocesan College, acted as secretary. We decided to oppose any move to cancel or restructure the school scholarships and requested an opportunity to make representations to the trustees. This was granted and in June 1971 Sir Richard Luyt put our case to them in Oxford. He had been a Rhodes scholar at Trinity just before the war and had had a distinguished career, having been Governor-General of Guyana and since then Vice-Chancellor of the University of Cape Town. He did not succeed in dissuading them from their plan but as the will had been embodied in a British Act of Parliament, legislation was necessary to amend its terms, which would involve considerable expense. To use the funds of the Rhodes Trust to pay for this legislation required the blessing of the Secretary of State for Education, who at that time was Margaret Thatcher. Fortunately for the schools, she declined the trustees' request. In advance she had visited South Africa to open the new telescope at Sutherland which was a joint British and South African venture and at an embassy cocktail party the opportunity was created for me to have a short discussion with her, during which she gave a clear indication of her thinking. It was not necessary for me to say anything. Needless to say I was delighted and went over to talk to her husband Denis, whom I knew was interested in rugby. So the school scholarships survived.

Although not claiming to be neutral on the issue I thought the above result was entirely right. There was quite insufficient justification for changing Rhodes' clearly expressed direction that Bishops should have a scholarship, as also the other three schools.

The 80th anniversary of the scholarships in 1983 was celebrated in style (as the British know how) with three days of events at Oxford, including a Garden Party at Rhodes House, visited by the Queen and the Duke of Edinburgh; a black tie dinner in an enormous marquee in the Trinity College garden; and dinners at each college for the Rhodes scholars of those colleges. At the black tie dinner in Trinity Harold Macmillan spoke in his capacity of University Chancellor. Until he spoke he had sat at the main table looking old and hardly up to making a speech but once on his feet he showed the same clarity and flair and expressive gestures I had witnessed when he made his 'wind of change' speech in Cape Town twenty-three years earlier. Julian Ogilvie Thompson replied on behalf of the Rhodes scholars. As described by Tim Nuttall in a chapter in *The History of the Rhodes Trust*, Ogilvie Thompson was in a business sense a direct descendant of Rhodes. He was deputy-chairman of both Anglo American and de Beers. He had been a Bishops Rhodes scholar at Worcester in the mid-1950s and had worked in the mining houses since then.

When we were summoned to get seated at the dinner our places had been set for us and my place was at the same fairly long table as my wife but when Verity got to her place she found herself a bit isolated as there was noone sitting on either side of her. After a couple of minutes a nearby incumbent told her with sensitivity that the places next to her had been earmarked for two American Rhodes scholars but that they had gone elsewhere in order not to sit next to an apartheid South African! Bearing in mind our active opposition to apartheid it seemed a bit over the top but we had an entertaining dinner.

At the Garden Party my wife and I, together with our son Philip, a current Rhodes Scholar, had the privilege of being presented to the Queen and the Duke of Edinburgh.

A controversial note was struck during the plenary session of the reunion's "general conference" at the Sheldonian.

Verity and I, and our son Philip, being presented to the Queen and the Duke of Edinburgh at the Rhodes Scholars reunion at Rhodes House, 1983.

An American Rhodes scholar who had figured in the 1971 campaign against the school scholarships and was now an attorney in Washington, got up to complain that despite the reforms to create

South-Africa-at-Large scholarships South Africa had only produced two black Rhodes scholars, one an Indian.

Critics of the failure to produce black Rhodes scholars via the South-Africa-at-large scholarships did not appreciate how difficult it was, with the inferior education system for blacks in South Africa, for selection committees to elect black scholars. Few applied and those that did were mostly not of a standard academically to meet Oxford's entrance requirements.

The controversy about the South African scholarships went quiet for a while but was revived again in the second half of the 1980s, partly by current Rhodes scholars but also by the American Association of Rhodes scholars. Britain's Race Relations Act of 1976 had provided them with an additional argument against discrimination. In 1987 the Rhodes trustees initiated legal proceedings to set aside the scholarships of Paul Roos and SACS. Bishops and St Andrews were by this time taking advantage of a more flexible government attitude and taking black scholars but the other two, being government schools, could not do so. The trustees' action was defended by the two schools and dragged on to the end of the decade, when the dramatic release of Nelson Mandela transformed the political scene and the trustees withdrew their case.

When the centenary of the scholarships came round in 2003 South Africa was no longer a pariah state and double celebrations were arranged in Cape Town in January and in England in July. Over 450 scholars came to Cape Town and over 800 attended the London and Oxford reunion. In Cape Town there was a Mayor's reception at Groot Constantia; a dinner at Boschendal, one of the Rhodes fruit farms near Stellenbosch owned by Anglo American, and another at Vergelegen at Somerset West, also owned by Anglo. There were tours to Robben Island; to the wild flower garden of Kirstenbosch and to the black townships; and lectures and conference discussions at the University of Cape Town. It was a very successful celebration.

The London celebration started with a gathering in Westminster Hall at which in addition to speeches by the Chairman of the Rhodes Trustees, Lord Waldegrave, and the Chancellor of Oxford University, Chris Patten, there were speeches by Nicky Oppenheimer, Chairman of de Beers, Bill Clinton , Tony Blair and Nelson Mandela , who had recently given his name and patronage to a Mandela Rhodes Foundation, created to assist African scholars. From London we went to further celebrations at Oxford.

At a dinner at University College for Univ Rhodes Scholars my wife and I sat at the same table as Bill and Hillary Clinton, Bob Hawke, Prime Minister of Australia, and Lord Robin Butler, Master of Univ. Bill Clinton was friendly and lively, Hillary more serious, seemingly with other things on her mind. I was sitting opposite her but the table was quite wide and I hesitated to try to talk to her above the noise of the conversations.

Bill and Hilary Clinton with Lord Butler, Master of University College, during the Rhodes Scholars reunion in 2003.

22

Helen Suzman's Memorial

*I*n March 2009, a month after Helen Suzman died, a memorial celebration was held in the Great Hall of the Witwatersrand University in Johannesburg. Earlier in Cape Town fifteen or twenty of her close associates in the Progressive Party had got together in Colin Eglin's house to remember her. At that stage we knew an appropriate memorial was planned in Johannesburg but Verity and I did not intend to go up for it. However when we  were contacted on behalf of Helen's family we decided to go, notwithstanding the distance. We were very glad we did, because it was a memorable occasion, a special gathering of people who had supported Helen in her opposition to apartheid. Moreover, when Colin spoke, he noted that of the original Progressive Party caucus of twelve in 1959, three were still alive: he, Ray Swart and myself, and the three of us were present. The audience responded warmly when he said this.

Helen's father and mother came to South Africa from Eastern Europe. She was born in Germiston in 1917 and she married a physician,

Dr Mosie Suzman. She studied at Wits and she went on to teach Economic History there. In 1953 she was persuaded to stand for the United Party for the parliamentary seat of Houghton and she held the Houghton seat for 36 years until she retired from parliament in 1989, just before Nelson Mandela was released from prison and the ANC and the PAC were unbanned. In 1959 she was one of the twelve MPs who left the United Party and started the Progressive Party under the leadership of Dr Jan Steytler. At the next general election in 1961 she was the only Progressive to be re-elected and she remained the sole Progressive in parliament for 13 years until she was joined by six other Progressive MPs in 1974. The Progressive Party later became the official opposition.

Mrs Frances Jowell, Helen's elder daughter, welcomed everyone on behalf of her sister and herself and said a few words about her mother, in particular how she had tenaciously pursued every request for assistance by people who needed help, of which there were many. Helen had insisted on her phone number remaining listed and the phone calls had come frequently and at all hours. She could not always achieve anything but she always tried. That was a theme repeated by other speakers, some of whom had personal experience of her help.

The Chancellor of Wits University, Judge Dikgang Moseneke, was a case in point. He recalled that as a young activist he and others had been prosecuted and sentenced to ten years imprisonment, without any violence having been proved, and Helen had recorded her disgust in parliament. She had regularly visited them in prison. She had supported his right to study while in prison, which had enabled him to become a lawyer and to hold the position he now held, Deputy Chief Justice. He recalled also how Robert Sobukwe, leader of the Pan Africanist Congress, had served a sentence imposed on him but when he was due to be released an Act was passed in parliament giving it the right to extend his detention for another year at a time. This Helen had strenuously opposed each year for eight years, arguing that noone should be detained without being tried by a court, which parliament was not, and that Sobukwe's protest against unjust laws should never have been a crime in the first place. Judge Moseneke recalled further that Helen had each year visited the Rivonia trialists on Robben Island: Nelson Mandela; Govan Mbeki , Walter Sisulu and others and had insisted on seeing the cells in which they were held.

Colin Eglin, leader of the Progressive Party for some years and a significant contributor to the Codesa negotiations of 1992 to 1994 which produced our new constitution, knew Helen better than any other speaker, having worked closely with her for more than 50 years. He said Helen was not just a great parliamentarian but more than a parliamentarian, a political activist who with great courage in a hostile parliament used it to get her message across and to expose injustice wherever she saw it. She went everywhere to see for herself, into the townships, into the shanty towns, into the prisons, and she knew her facts. She was lucid in her arguments; no obfuscation; no spin. He recalled with pleasure how in 1986, when the pass laws were repealed, something she had fought for from the time she entered parliament, two young Nationalists had crossed the floor of the House of Assembly and congratulated her. Among other things he recalled that Helen had been very impressed by what she described as inspiring words by Robert Kennedy in Cape Town in 1966 in concluding his address to students of the University of Cape Town:

> "Few will have the greatness to bend history itself but each of us can work to change a small portion of events and in the total of all those acts will be written the history of this generation. It is from numberless, diverse acts of courage and belief that human history is shaped. Each time a man stands up for an ideal or acts to improve the lot of others, or strikes out against injustice, he sends forth a tiny ripple of hope, and crossing each other from a million different sources of energy and daring, those ripples build a current which can sweep down the mightiest walls of oppression."

Helen reproduced these words of Robert Kennedy in her memoirs *In No Uncertain Terms*. She and Colin had helped him with the arrangements for his visit to South Africa. After his address to the UCT students Kennedy went to Colin's house for the evening and I and a few others were fortunate to be able to take part in the evening's informal discussion.

An anecdote from Ann Bernstein, a researcher who often accompanied Helen into the townships, typified her refusal to be intimidated and her ability to give back as good as she got. After Helen returned to parliament in 1961 as the sole Progressive Dr Verwoerd said to her across the House "I have written you off". Helen replied: "The whole world has written you off"!

We next heard from Archbishop Desmond Tutu, speaking in his inimitable style and with his showman's flair. He gave Helen generous praise: "this feisty, petite lady, who stood up to the jeers of the Nationalists in parliament with quite remarkable determination and courage, the only real opposition to the ghastliness of apartheid". Having complimented her he took advantage of the occasion to direct some trenchant points at the ANC government: that power was for service and there should be zero tolerance for corruption. He said we had an impressive array of talent in the country, which was for all of us, and noone should be sidelined. "If we got it right" (I have paraphrased) "we are a scintillating success waiting to happen".

Like Archbishop Tutu, Dr Mamphela Ramphele used the example of Helen's service ethic to express her concern at the incidents of corruption and culture of impunity which were manifesting themselves in our public life. Government was for service, not for enrichment, she said. Dr Ramphele's history is perhaps less well known than the other speakers. She was a medical doctor, one of the few black doctors in the country, and was a close friend of Steve Biko and the mother of his child. She and Biko were founder members of the Black Consciousness Movement. Biko was banned and later killed by inhuman treatment in detention and Dr Ramphele was banned and restricted to a remote area in the northern Transvaal, where she ran a medical and community service for the people of the district. After Nationalist rule ended she was appointed Vice-Chancellor of the University of Cape Town. In 2000 she was appointed managing director of the International Bank for Reconstruction and Development at the World Bank. Her criticisms could not be written off as racist, any more than Archbishop Tutu's.

In addition to the chairmanship of John Kane-Berman, on behalf of the Institute of Race Relations, a poem by Danny Jowell, grandson of Helen, and a cameo by Evita Bezuidenhout, the alter ego of the satirist Pieter Dirk Uys, we also enjoyed interesting tributes from Chief

Mangosuthu Buthelezi, Nicky Oppenheimer and Helen Zille, Premier of the Western Cape Provincial Government and leader of the Democratic Alliance, the successor to the Progressive Party, which runs Cape Town Municipality and the Western Cape.

At the end of the tributes an impressive Wits choir sang the national anthem and continued with their singing while the dignitaries left the

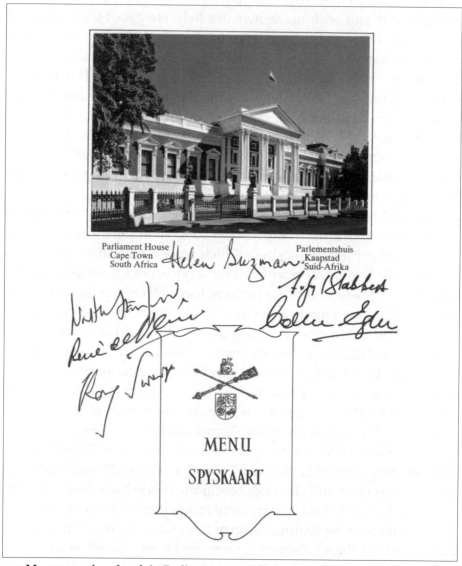

Menu cover for a lunch in Parliament to celebrate Helen Suzman's 30 years in parliament. The signatures are of Helen, van Zyl Slabbert, Colin Eglin, Ray Swart, Rene de Villiers and Walter Stanford.

hall. The latter included ex-President Thabo Mbeki and his wife; Graca Machel, wife of Nelson Mandela; and representatives of a number of foreign embassies. Nelson was not able to be present. He and Graca had paid a special visit to the Suzman family after Helen's death.

Our son Mark lives in Johannesburg with his family. He lectured in Civil Engineering at Wits for some years and was pleased to escort Verity and me to the memorial and to experience it with us.

MRS HELEN SUZMAN, M P

L U N C H E O N
Friday, 15 April 1983

30 YEARS IN PARLIAMENT

Master of Ceremonies   Ray Swart, M P
Toast   Colin Eglin, M P

WINES

Nederburg Paarl Riesling
Nederburg Paarl Cabernet
****
Sweet Melon Gallant Lady
*****
Mushroom Veloute Blue Haze
*****
Fried kabeljou Houghton Girls with tartar sauce
*****
Bobotie Harvard and rice
Rolled loin of mutton Oxford with mint sauce
*****
Vegetables a la Mosie
*****
Chicken Louis Steyn Ox tongue Bensusan Polony Senekal
*****
Civil Liberties Salads
*****
13 Lonely years Chocolate pudding
Cold Jimmy Ice cream
OR
Mixed Sweets
*****
Fruits of Perseverance
*****
Mature 90 day Cheese and biscuits
*****
Black or White coffee
*****
30 Year Port Wine

The Menu itself, which included Cold Jimmy Ice Cream,
Mature 90-day Cheese and Biscuits as well as Black or White coffee!

23

Cricket after 50 years

*T*he 2010/2011 season in the southern hemisphere saw two fine test match series between England and Australia in Australia and between India and South Africa in South Africa, confirming to purists like myself that the five-day form of the game is still the most interesting.

It was appropriate that we should have had a tour by an Indian team this summer because it is 150 years since the first group of Indians settled in South Africa. There were two examples at Newlands of the contribution they have made in our country: Hashim Amla on the field and Haroon Lorgat, CEO of the ICC, a guest in the President's suite.

The Indian and South African teams were first and second in the international ranking but the series between England and Australia was of at least equal interest because England and Australia are the two oldest cricket-playing countries and their rivalry has been legendary. The big crowds at Melbourne and Sydney contributed to the atmosphere.

Then there was the 50 overs World Cup, with India worthy winners. South Africa had a bad day in their quarter-final against New Zealand and came in for some strong criticism, which in my view was overdone. In a limited overs game you have to take more risks than in a test match and things can easily go wrong. But I think my more tolerant reaction was a minority view in South Africa.

In my time, when one lost, one could say that it was only a game. Today it is much more of a business. The change was well described by my godson Vincent van der Bijl, who played first-class cricket from

1968 to 1983. He was chosen for the South African team to tour Australia in 1971 but the tour was called off and although he was an
outstanding fast bowler (as his season for Middlesex showed) South
Africa's isolation from international cricket denied him the chance to
play an official test match. Soon after he retired in 1983 he wrote a book
Cricket in the Shadows (co-authored by John Bishop, Sports Editor of the
Natal Witness) in which he described how in his relatively short playing
career the game had changed from one where the interests of cricket
were paramount to one ruled by business needs. The amateur player
was now being paid and had his union; the administrator had changed
from unpaid part-time worker to businessman; and the sponsors were
forcing changes in order to get a return on the money they were
spending.

I was reminded of the influence of business when watching the test
match against the Indians at Newlands over the New Year. When I
played in the 1950s there was no business name to be seen at Newlands. In 2011 there is hardly a surface on which a business is not
advertised, even the rooves of the stands. The boundary is a rope about
a meter in from the fence round the field, which is sensible, but all 360
degrees of the fence are covered with advertisements, many of them
changing every few minutes to catch one's eye, or to advertise an additional name. Even the sightscreens display an advertisement when the
bowling is from the other end. Newlands' very name has changed to
Sahara Park Newlands.

What else has changed? Limited overs cricket, of the 50 overs variety, has been a very successful innovation, though too many games are
sometimes added at the end of a test series. 20/20 cricket has its following but I am not a fan.

The first time I saw television was in our changing room at the Oval
in the fifth test, 1951. Television broadcasting has been developed to a
fine art.

The use of cameras, hawk-eye and hotspot have been interesting
developments, helping to eliminate bad decisions and adding considerable interest for spectators. Bell survived a faint snick in the Sydney
test because hot-spot did not pick it up (although "snicko" did) which
confirms that these aids are not infallible. I wonder whether hawk-eye
is entirely reliable, particularly when the ball hits the batsman's front

leg, because one often sees a ball swing after it has pitched, which hawk-eye can't predict. India was opposed to the use of hawk-eye and hot-spot in South Africa this season, but they are surely a positive development. Likewise the review system.

Technology and the review system put umpires right in the spotlight. They have shown what excellent international umpires we have. The practice of having "neutral" umpires in international matches, not umpires of the host country, as in my day, is obviously better and the development of a panel of international umpires has been good. I see from the last annual report of the ICC that they are sponsored by the Emirates and that there were 12 umpires on the "Emirates Elite Panel" last year. My favourite umpires at present are Aleem Dar and Simon Taufel, for their calm authority, followed by Billy Bowden for his eccentric signalling.

The invented term "reverse-swing" is something of a misnomer, because whether the ball swings in or out will depend on how you hold it and bowl it, not on how you bowled it earlier. However, shining one side of the ball and keeping the other side rough has increased as a tactic and helps it to swing. Making the one side rough has, at times, been taken to extremes but that is another story.

Helmets; coaches for international teams (sometimes three, for batting, bowling and fielding); high-fives and drinks at the fall of a wicket (or the drop of a hat); bats with straight edges; presentations after the game; reverse sweeps; etc: the list of "advances" is quite long.

In 1931, on his 80th birthday, Lord Harris famously wrote to *The Times* commending cricket to young English sportsmen. "You do well to love it (he wrote) for it is more free from anything sordid, anything dishonourable, than any game in the world. To play it keenly, honourably, generously, self-sacrificingly is a moral lesson in itself, and the classroom is God's air and sunshine".

Eighty years later the MCC's World Cricket Committee has felt the need to set up an Anti-Corruption sub-committee led by Steve Waugh and including Courtney Walsh and Barry Richards and the ICC also has an Anti-Corruption and Security unit.

But the spirit of cricket has been largely upheld.

The control of cricket has moved from the MCC to the ICC, with its headquarters in Dubai. The ICC was formed as the Imperial Cricket

Conference as long ago as 1912, when there were just three members, England, Australia and South Africa, and its powers were very limited. Its name is now International Cricket Council. Haroon Lorgat told me recently that the number of full and associate member countries was 105! In this democratic age it would not be tenable for the MCC to be the controlling body of cricket and the ICC looks to be doing a professional job in "promoting and protecting the game, and its unique spirit" (from its mission statement). There was a charm in cricket being controlled by the MCC from Lord's, which in a sense I miss. The MCC does remain the custodian of the laws of cricket and Lord's is still the Mecca of cricket.

Scrapbook items

1. Oxford v Cambridge at Twickenham, December 1948.

2. England v Scotland at Twickenham, March 1949.

3. Second day's play, Gentlemen v Players, Lord's, July 1949.

4. Ex-captains at Hansie Cronje's benefit dinner.

5. Receiving the Mayor's Medal for services to Sport and Recreation.

THRILLING WIN FOR OXFORD

From Our Rugby Football Correspondent

Oxford won a thrilling match at Twickenham yesterday by seizing their chances. At half-time they led by 11 points to none, but then followed a great rally by Cambridge which, with a little more luck, might well have brought them level, or even ahead. Finally, Van Ryneveld, one of the Oxford centres, after clearing his lines with one long kick ahead, got in two more and ended up by scoring the decisive try in the last 10 minutes. In this way Oxford gained a hard-earned victory by one goal, one dropped goal, and two tries (14 points) to one goal and one penalty goal (8 points).

All University Rugby matches, of course, are hard and fast and exciting. This one, however, approached greatness because both sides showed a cut-and-thrust which nothing short of the most determined marking and tackling could parry. Oxford only succeeded because, in spite of the fact that their heavier forwards did not give them quite the advantage generally expected in the tight, backs and forwards alike showed the necessary enterprise and team-work even when things were going badly. The intensity of the Cambridge attacks—not only in the second half—would have broken most teams. Oxford not merely held out; they forced Cambridge to make the mistakes in handling and running which alone explained why the Oxford line was not crossed more than once—one very nearly wrote repeatedly—during the period when the whole game hung in the balance.

True to tradition and wise expectation, the game was full of surprising things. One was quite prepared, for instance, for Hofmeyr's valuable tactical kicking from the stand-off position; even, perhaps, for his dropped goal; but not for the brilliant break-through which, admirably supported, first, by Stewart, the full-back, and then by the two forwards, Vintcent and Gill, brought Oxford their first try after about 24 minutes' play. Gill moved up on the left flank in the manner of a wing three-quarter and Stewart completed the whole move by adding the goal points from the widest of angles. Apart from this, Stewart was rather disappointing except, perhaps, when he moved up to help his centres. On the day, Holmes, the Cambridge full-back, was his superior but, admittedly, Holmes had to play a fine game in order to achieve that distinction.

THE CAMBRIDGE TRY

And who could possibly have expected the one Cambridge try to come from a shove which pushed the Oxford pack right off the ball ? Dorward, who improved as the game proceeded, was able to pick the ball up unhurriedly and throw a long reverse pass to his partner. Glyn Davies thereupon seized his best chance with a speed and sidestep which might have beaten the finest defence. For the most part Davies and his fellow backs tried in vain to penetrate the rock-like defence confronting them. At least they did bravely to keep on attacking with such fire, in spite of the heavy tackling to which they were subjected.

Cambridge went off with a bang at the start and were only beaten back to their own " 25 " by good kicking. Thereabouts, just after Stewart had failed with a penalty kick at goal, Hofmeyr caught the drop-out and placed his side ahead with a dropped goal at least worth the three points now allowed by the laws. Gloag and Smith were prominent in the Cambridge attacks which followed, attacks which failed largely because the passing and running were not clever enough to overcome a sound defence. Hofmeyr's breakaway and the try which attended it was the next shock administered to a confident Cambridge, closely followed by a third, when Cannell, Swarbrick, and Van Ryneveld, flattered a little by shaky tackling, set up the attack which enabled the last-mentioned to score Oxford's second try. This Stewart could not make into a goal.

Eleven points down, Cambridge returned to the attack, but still without any success.

There were 15 minutes of intense excitement in the second half before the magnificent efforts of the Cambridge forwards were effectively supported by the backs. Davies's try, converted into a goal by Holmes, made the whole of the crowd of some 40,000 people feel that the game was far from being lost and won yet. This impression was confirmed by the penalty goal kicked by Holmes from 50 yards range about five minutes later—for another case of barging in the line-out. But although Cambridge persisted and four times got within a yard or so of success—once only a superb tackle got Smith by the heels—they were fated to fall further behind instead of drawing level or going ahead. C. B. Van Ryneveld's decisive effort no doubt came about by chance, but it was a chance splendidly seized at the end of a series of long kicks ahead, the last of which sent the ball rolling almost into touch-in-goal. Holmes had been badly caught out of position and Scott had tried in vain to fall on the ball before the final kick ahead. The race went on and Van Ryneveld must have covered nearly 100 yards before he just won it.

The game did not die even then, but it was now a forlorn hope indeed for Cambridge and even Smith's last dash for the line could not have saved them.

ENGLAND'S SECOND VICTORY

From Our Rugby Football Correspondent

England ended their international season in a blaze of March sunshine and belated glory at Twickenham on Saturday, when they beat Scotland by two goals and three tries (19 points) to one penalty goal (three points). The Duke of Edinburgh was present to see the match.

It was, perhaps, more a great occasion than a great match, but at least England played with the same dash and determination which, three weeks earlier, had enabled them to beat France on the same ground. In doing so, moreover, England not only recovered the Calcutta Cup—that modern gauge of battle; one to make the old borderers lick their lips—but

INTERNATIONAL TABLE

			P.	W.	L.	F.	A.	Points
IRELAND	..	..	4	3	1	41	24	6
ENGLAND	..	..	4	2	2	35	29	4
SCOTLAND	..	..	4	2	2	20	37	4
FRANCE	..	..	3	1	2	19	25	2
WALES	..	..	3	1	2	14	14	2

flung back the wooden spoon in the faces of all those who had still feared the worst would happen again. Altogether, England were worthy as well as decisive winners. Had they made a similar effort in Dublin after taking the lead there, the championship table would now have looked very different.

But, then, who could have imagined that the same Scots who had won so gallantly against France and Wales would end up so tamely against their oldest traditional opponents? Admittedly, they were only 14 effectives much of the time. It can be said with some show of truth that, if they never really looked like a winning side, they only became a losing one from the moment Jackson was seen to be limping badly and no longer able to hold Kennedy on the English left wing. Hitherto, he had done so with giant ease, once nearly flinging his man into the west stand. Thenceforward—England having scored the only try of the first half 10 minutes before the interval—Scotland tried in vain to remedy matters by swift exchanges of Jackson and Smith whenever a spacious open side promised the chance of an effective passing movement and Jackson could be left in charge of a short, unused blind side. It did not work out all for Scotland. Other measures would have been much wiser.

A lively ball and the pronounced tendency of both sets of backs to pass a full stride or so too soon vitiated a lot of open play which otherwise might have become really exciting. The forwards and scrum-halves—the latter even under the shadow of the spoiler—served their fellows generously. Scotland seldom emerged for more than a moment or so from their own half of the field, but, during the first 40 minutes, at any rate, they had a fair share of the ball. There, however, the terms of equality ended abruptly. In attack, only the two powerful Scottish wings looked at all threatening, and they were easily marked. Preece and all four English three-quarters, in spite of their extremely moderate passing, were individually full of dash and enterprise. This and the growing strength of the forwards told more and more in the second half when Scotland were almost routed—certainly outplayed.

Apart from the inability of Holmes to land some penalty points for England from 30 yards at an angle, with little wind for or against, there was a surprising scarcity of near-things up to the interval. England's numerous attacks only brought results when, suddenly, Roberts—liveliest of all the English forwards from start to finish—broke clean away in the loose and reached the opposing full-back before passing out to Van Ryneveld. The latter, with commendable judgment, handed on almost at once to an unmarked Kennedy, whose splendid dash did the rest. The angle was too wide for Holmes to add the goal points.

The second half had a remarkable beginning. The Scots opened one of their rather laborious passing movements, only to be shocked by a swift counter-attack in which the ever-watchful Preece followed up his own punt-ahead and passed to Van Ryneveld. The latter always is ready for a " go " given half a chance, and on this occasion, with the aid of a dummy, he writhed his way through a crowded but bemused defence and finally dived over the goal-line in the manner of the storybooks. Travers was brought up to convert a thrilling try into a more prosaic but exceedingly useful goal—all the more valuable when, barely a minute later, Wilson kicked a penalty goal for Scotand from 35 yards wide out.

This kept Scotland just in the running—but only just—for another 10 minutes. Then, after yet another Scottish passing move had been broken up, the English halves, in a rather confused situation, offered Van Ryneveld his

second chance. This he took, again with help of a dummy, and although Travers's kick at goal hit a post England now led 11 points to 3. The forwards, more than then took up the running and Hosking c pleted a strong breakaway by Vaug Travers added the goal points, and with than a quarter of an hour left for play match was as good as over. The English in reality had done even more than their b to ensure victory. There was hardly perilous Scottish rush, and Keller's iso breakaway were of small account.

Scotland, however, were not spared a English try, the result of a brilliant cut-thr —one of several deserving efforts—by Can who virtually reached the goal-line be giving a short scoring pass to Guest. Tr made a creditable attempt to kick a goal f the touch-line, but the margin of 19 p to 3 was ample to rehabilitate England more than enough to deprive Scotland of honour of sharing the championship with land. Many of the great crowd no doub the ground pondering deeply on the vag of Rugby form and the mysteries of hu endeavour. The thoughts of Welshmen Frenchmen present—not to mention any —can only be imagined.

The teams were : —

ENGLAND.—W. B. Holmes (Cambridge Unive R. H. Guest (Waterloo), L. B. Cannell (Oxford U sity), C. B. Van Ryneveld (Oxford University), Kennedy (Camborne School of Mines); J. (Coventry) (captain), W. K. T. Moore (Leice J. McG. Kendall-Carpenter (Oxford University), Steeds (Middlesex Hospital), T. W. Price (Chelten G. R. D'A. Hosking (Devonport Services), J. Matthews (Harlequins), V. G. Roberts (Penryn), Vaughan (Headingley), B. H. Travers (Harlequin

SCOTLAND.—I. J. M. Lumsden (R.A.F.); I. Jackson (London Scottish), L. G. Gloag (Cam University), D. P. Hepburn (Woodford), D. W. C (London Scottish); C. R. Bruce (Glasgow Academ W. D. Allardice (Aberdeen G.S.F.P.); S. T. V (Stewart's College F.P.), J. A. R. MacPhail (Edin Academicals), S. Coltman (Hawick), L. R. Currie fermline), G. A. Wilson (Oxford University), T Keller (London Scottish), P. W. Kininmonth (C University), W. I. D. Elliot (Edinburgh Academic

REFEREE.—N. H. Lambert (Ireland).

CRICKET

KEEN STRUGGLE AT LORD'S

THE GENTLEMEN RECOVER

From Our Cricket Correspondent

The Gentlemen made a fair recovery in their second innings against the Players at Lord's yesterday, and at the close of play were 113 runs ahead with two wickets yet to fall. A slender lead, no doubt, but most commendable after the tribulations they had been through.

For this they were indebted to Bailey and Van Ryneveld, who added 115 runs for the sixth wicket, and explained what some other batsmen seem to have forgotten, or not realized, that the best way of playing spin bowling on a fast wicket is to get to the pitch of the ball.

Already 50 runs ahead with four wickets to fall the Players, in the morning, were in a position with two such adventurous batsmen as Close and Evans still in, to force the pace. Eighteen runs, however, had only been added when Evans, trying to hit a ball to leg, cocked it up to give a catch at the wicket. Perks, in his free and easy way, cracked a few balls about to the delight of the crowd, but it was Close, who had batted so well from the moment that he went in on Wednesday evening, who was the run scorer. He has the full swing of a left-handed batsman, and for a young man of 18, playing in his first Gentlemen and Players match, this was a most commendable performance. He is quite clearly a cricketer of great promise.

The Gentlemen went in to bat at 10 minutes to 1, 129 runs behind, and for many overs Dewes looked uncertain and uncomfortable in his stroke play to the bowling of Perks and Jackson. Compton, not satisfied, tried a combination of spin with Hollies and Jenkins, the latter of whom had not bowled an over in the first innings. Luncheon arrived without the fall of a wicket, and afterwards Dewes was an entirely different player, now meeting the ball with the full face of the bat and once making a lovely square drive off the back foot from the bowling of Hollies. He was granted, too, a full pitch by Close, which he hit straight for 4.

EARLY WICKETS

Simpson in the meantime was playing surely enough, yet finding great difficulty in discovering a gap on the off side when batting to Hollies. Once he did find it, so a man was moved back to deep extra cover, but with the score at 54 Simpson, playing forward, was caught at fine short leg. With Edrich in, Jenkins was brought on in place of Hollies, and the width and sharpness of break which Jenkins commanded was at once a disturbing factor. He had Edrich stumped when stretching out to the ball, and at 65 Doggart, also leaning out, was caught at the wicket.

Nine runs later Dewes, who had just hit a ball from Close to the square-leg boundary, in trying to repeat the stroke off Jenkins was beaten by the break and bowled. Yardley was treated to one full pitch which he dispatched to the boundary before he was leg-before-wicket trying to turn a ball to leg, and so half the side was out and they were still 44 runs behind.

There followed the stand between Van Ryneveld and Bailey, built carefully and adroitly. Bailey started his scoring with a sweep to leg off Jenkins for four all run, and with Van Ryneveld playing truly down the line of the ball, Compton, with the score at 111, gave himself a turn of bowling. It was not long, however, before the attack was again handed over to Hollies and Jenkins, neither of whom offered the batsmen many chances of scoring.

The new ball with Perks and Jackson on again caused little discomfort to the batsmen, with Perks at first bowling many balls so wide of the leg stump that it required all the agility of Evans to save four byes on several occasions. Gradually Bailey and Van Ryneveld—Bailey in particular—were transforming what had been little more than resistance to definite attack, though Van Ryneveld, when 34, was missed by Evans from a ball off Jackson which he might have left to short slip to take. The respective rate of scoring of the two was level in quality and steady in quantity, with Van Ryneveld driving the ball to the on whenever he felt it pitched up sufficiently and Bailey always ready to push it away to leg or hit it to the least strongly guarded portion of the off side.

With the bowling still regular in length and often vicious in spin this batting was of a high order, and together they had taken the score to 200 when Hollies, with a ball which came straight through, had Van Ryneveld leg-before-wicket. In the natural sequence of circumstances after a long stand Bailey was out 15 runs later, also leg-before-wicket, and at 219 Brown was stumped, Evans gathering the ball well on the leg side.

But this was by no means the end of the Gentlemen's challenge, for their captain came in to play many a rich stroke, as Bailey had done before, quick in his decision to get to the pitch of the ball.

Score:—

GENTLEMEN.—First Innings, 105 (Hollies 5 for 32).

SECOND INNINGS

J. G. Dewes, b. Jenkins	..	33
R. T. Simpson, c. Langridge (John), b. Close	..	28
W. J. Edrich, st. Evans, b. Jenkins	..	4
G. H. G. Doggart, c. Evans, b. Jenkins	..	4
N. W. D. Yardley, l.-b.-w., b. Jenkins	..	9
C. B. Van Ryneveld, l.-b.-w., b. Hollies	..	64
T. E. Bailey, l.-b.-w., b. Hollies	..	53
F. G. Mann, not out	..	34
F. R. Brown, st. Evans, b. Hollies	..	2
A. H. Kardar, not out	..	1
Extras	..	10
Total (for 8 wkts.)	..	242

PLAYERS.—First Innings

Hutton, c. Edrich, b. Brown	..	25
Langridge (John), l.-b.-w., b. Bailey	..	31
Robertson, b. Bailey	..	1
Compton (D.), l.-b.-w., b. Yardley	..	33
Graveney (T. W.), c. Kardar, b. Brown	..	2
Close, c. Simpson, b. Brown	..	65
Jenkins, b. Bailey	..	5
Evans, c. Griffith, b. Brown	..	41
Perks, c. Dewes, b. Brown	..	13
Hollies, c. Bailey, b. Kardar	..	5
Jackson (L.), not out	..	8
Extras (l.b. 2, n.b. 3)	..	5
Total	..	234

BOWLING.—First Innings.—Bailey, 22—4—59—3; Edrich, 9—1—30—0; Brown, 24.4—1—80—5; Yardley, 10—3—18—1; Van Ryneveld, 3—0—17—0; Kardar, 5—1—25—1.

Ex-captains at Hansie Cronje's benefit dinner at Bloemfontein, late 1990s.
Back-row: Tiffie Barnes, Ali Bacher, Hansie Cronje, Clive Rice, Khaya Majola.
Seated: Peter van der Merwe, Basil D'Oliveira, Trevor Goddard, CvR.

Receiving the Mayor's Medal for Services to Sport and Recreation from Helen Zille 2009.

Index

A

Aaron, Sam 154
Abed, Dik 70
Abrahams, Cecil 70
Ackerman, Hylton 70-71
Adcock, Neil 112-117, 119, 123, 128, 131, 134, 136-137
Alington, Giles 20
Allen, David Ravern 73
Altham, Harry 64, 78
Alvarez, Andre 25, 45
Amla, Hashim 184
Andrew, Rob 162
Arlott, John 40, 68-69, 72, 73-74, 77, 102
Attlee, Clement 19, 108

B

Bacher, Ali 158, 160, 170, 192
Bader, Leslie 152
Bailey, Trevor 35, 58, 122, 123, 125-126, 129-130, 171
Balaskas, X 80
Bam, Gert 164
Bannister, Roger 62
Barlow, Eddie 70, 169
Bartlett, John 54
Basquet, Guy 46
Bayley, Peter 20
Beck, JEF 113
Bedser, Alec 99, 101
Benaud, Richie 78, 89, 134-136, 157
Bernstein, Ann 181
Beveridge, Sir William 19
Bickerton, Fred 20
Biehl, Amy 167

Biko, Steve 181
Birkett, Sir Norman 64
Blair, Tony 176
Blanckenberg, Jimmy 12, 70
Boobbyer, Brian 61
Bowden, Billy 186
Boycott, Geoff 171
Boyes, Robert 14
Bradman, Sir Donald 33-34, 66, 100, 168
Brennan, DV 32
Brittenden, RT 116
Brown, Freddie 34, 58-59, 98, 103-104
Brown, WA 33
Burke, JW 134
Burton, Paul 95
Butcher, Ronald 141
Buthelezi, Chief Mangosuthu 182
Butler, Lord Robin 19, 177

C

Cagwe, Ezra 166
Cahn, Sir Julien 78
Cameron, Jock 66, 80
Campbell, Iain 56
Cannell, Lewis 37, 39, 47, 49, 61
Cardus, Sir Neville 75-77, 106
Carlstein, Peter 136
Carpmael, William 49
Carr, Donald 53, 61
Carter, Eddie 157
Chappell, Greg 157
Chapple, ME 112, 114
Cheetham, Jack 15, 94, 97, 111-112, 114, 116, 121-122, 169
Chester, Frank 66

Chesterton, George 53-54
Chubb, Geoff 97-98, 101, 104
Clinton, Bill v, 21, 176-177
Clinton, Hillary 177
Close, Brian 54, 58
Coetsee, Gert 154-155
Compton, Denis 35, 58-59, 68, 92, 98, 100,
    103-106, 122-123, 125-126, 128-131
Corbett, Mick 18, 154
Costello, V 124
Cowdrey, Colin 68, 78, 123, 126, 128, 162
Cowie, J 55
Craig, Ian 135, 171
Creese, Frank 90
Currie, Sir Donald 14, 86

D

Dar, Aleem 186
Davies, Dai 104
Davies, Glyn 37-38, 40-41
Day, Jeremy 160
Deane, Nummy 80
de Beer, Zach 138, 141
de Klerk, FW 109
Dewar, David 160
Dewes, John 56, 58
Doggart, Hubert 35, 56, 58, 64
Dollery, Tom 69
Donnelly, Martin 55-56, 59
Dorward, Arthur 37
Duffus, Louis 80, 106
Duke of Edinburgh 46, 67, 162, 174-175
Duncan, Graeme 152, 154
du Plessis, Morné 160
D'Oliveira, Basil 12, 70, 74, 90, 192

E

Earl of Lindsay 86
Eden, Anthony 108
Edrich, Bill 35, 58

Eglin, Colin 141, 147, 180
Elizabeth, Queen 67, 162-165, 174-175
Endean, Russell 97, 102, 104, 112-113,
    116-117, 124-125, 127-130, 132
Evans, Godfrey 58-59, 123, 126, 128

F

Fagan, Hannes 19
Farnes, Ken 13
Fellowes, Lord Robert 164
Fingleton, Jack 34, 81, 168
Fortune, Charles 80, 136
Friedman, Gerald 154
Fry, CB vi, 79
Fuller, Eddie 70, 117, 119
Fullerton, George 97
Funston, Ken 125

G

Gadney, Cyril 27
Galombik, Arnold 161
Gent, Nick 23, 61
Gibson, Jimmy 149
Gloag, LG 37, 39, 47
Goddard, Trevor 117, 122-123, 126, 128,
    131, 134-136, 192
Goodhart, Arthur 19
Goodman, Arnold 19
Gorvy, Harold 154-155
Graaff, Sir de Villiers 138, 141
Grace, WG 57
Graham, David 85
Graveney, Tom 53, 58
Greenhalgh, Peter 36
Greig, Tony 70
Griffith, Billy 58
Guest, Dickie 42, 44, 49
Gwilliam, JA 37

H

Hadlee, Walter 55, 59, 171
Haig Smith, Jack 49
Hall, Nim 41-42
Hammond, Wally 67
Hanley, Martin 15
Harris, Lord 186
Harris, Tony 15
Hartford, Gordon 149
Harvey, Neil 33, 135, 171
Hassett, Lindsay 31, 33-34, 94, 171
Hawke, Bob 177
Hawke, Lord 86
Heine, Peter 117, 119, 122-123, 125, 128, 131, 134, 136-137
Hendren, Denis 66
Hendriks, Rushdi 95
Hobbs, Jack 65-66
Hoffmann, Lord Leonard 19, 93
Hofmeyr, Murray 37-38, 54, 56
Hollies, WE 58
Holmes, Barry 37, 39, 47
Honore, Tony 21
Hopwood, Charles 50
Howa, Hassan 157
Hughes, Glyn 50
Hunter, Bishop John 139
Hutton, Len 31-32, 54, 58, 68-69, 79, 100-102, 104, 107, 124

I

Ikin, Jack 98, 101
Innes, Gerald 94
Insole, Doug 35, 56, 104, 122, 125, 130-131
Ironside, Dave 112, 114, 117
Irvine, Lee 70

J

Jackman, Robin 13

Jaffee, Gerald 152, 154
Jardine, Douglas 64
Jaxa, Felix 150
Jenkins, Roley 54, 58-59
Johnston, Bill 34
Johnston, Brian 83, 105, 160-161
Jones, Ken 40-41
Jones, Trevor 46
Jowell, Danny 181
Jowell, Frances 179

K

Kallis, Jacques 72
Kane-Berman, John 181
Kardar, Hafeez 31, 34-35, 53, 58-59
Keen, Ginger 15
Keighley, Geoffrey 34
Kendall-Carpenter, John 37, 47
Kennedy, Bob 49
Kennedy, Robert 180
Kgosana, Philip 145
Kimberley, HM 37
Kininmonth, Peter 47
Kirsten, Peter 71
Kline, Lindsay 89, 134
Knight, David 18
Koornhof, Dr 157
Kyle, Jack 41-42, 51

L

Laker, Jim 101, 103-104, 123-124
Lamb, Allan 71
Langley, GRA 94
Langridge, John 58
Lawrence, Harry 141
Leary, Stuart 70
Leigh, Vivien 108
Lewis, Tony 171
Liddle, Jimmy 117-118
Lindsay, DT 33-34, 169, 171

Lindwall, Ray 33, 78, 94, 105
Lloyd-Davies 26
Loader, PJ 123, 128, 129
Lock, GAR 23, 123, 128
Lorgat, Haroon 184, 187
Lowson, FA 102
Loxton, SJE 33-34
Luker, John 91
Luyt, Freddie 12
Luyt, Richard snr 12
Luyt, Sir Richard 174

M

Machel, Graca 183
Macmillan, Harold 108, 142, 144, 174
Macpherson, Tommy 28
Magiet, Rushdi 70
Mailey, Arthur 82
Majola, Khaya 160
Major, John 162
Makosana, Solomon 166
Malan, Basil 129
Malan, Dr DF 109, 138
Mallett, Tony 32, 35, 174
Mandela, Nelson 71, 154, 160, 170, 176,
    179, 183
Mann, George 58, 171
Mann, Tufty 15, 97, 99, 107
Mansell, Percy 97
Mars, Wally 91-93
Marsh, Norman 20
Martin-Jenkins, Christopher 83, 130
Matthews, Jackie 40
Maud, Sir John 19, 143
May, Peter iv-v, 41, 59, 68, 102, 122-123,
    125-126, 128, 143, 161, 171
Mbeki, Govan 179
Mbeki, Thabo 183
McCarthy, Cuan 97-98, 103
McCarthy, Jim 41, 52

McCarthy, Neil 160
McCool, Colin 33-34
McDonald, Colin 134, 137
McGibbon, Tony 112
McGilvray, Alan 83, 105
McGlew, Jackie 97, 112, 116-117,
    121-124, 134
McKay, Billy 41
McKee, Des 42, 51
McLean, Roy 97, 99, 116-117, 125-126,
    131, 136
Melle, Mike 97
Melville, Alan 14-15
Menzies, Sir Robert 82
Mguqulwa, Fezile 166
Miller, Keith 33, 105, 171
Miller, LSM 113
Millin, Douglas 21
Mills, Freddie 92
Mitchell, Bruce 15, 80
Mitchell, Douglas 140
Moga, Alban 41, 45
Molteno, Donald 142
Montgomery, Field Marshall 36
Mooney, Frank 112-114
Moore, W 42
Morris, Arthur 33
Morris, Bob 20
Moseneke, Judge Dikgang 179
Mullen, Karl 41

N

Neethling, Coetie 70
Nel, Jack 80, 84
Newman, Jack 13, 90, 93
Newman, Syd 26
Newton Thompson, Joyce 62
Newton Thompson, Ossie 24, 62
Njengele, Gerald 160, 166
Nourse, Dave 54

Nourse, Dudley 15, 80, 96-97, 99, 102-103, 107, 111
Nuffield, Lord 13

O

Odendaal, Andre 156, 160, 167
Ogilvie Thompson, Julian 174
Oppenheimer, Nicky 176, 182
Ovenstone, Dougie 15
Overton, GWF 114
Owen-Smith, Tuppy 84
O'Brien, Des 25, 41
O'Reilly, Tony 52

P

Passmore, John 94-95, 156, 158, 160-161, 167, 170
Patten, Chris 176
Pawson, Tony 31, 34-35, 64
Pegler, Syd 96, 106-107
Pithey, AJ 125
Plimsoll, Jack 15-16
Pollock, Graeme 168
Poore, MB 113
Prat, Jean 45
Preece, Ivor 42, 44-46
Procter, Mike 70

R

Rabinowitz, Benny 160
Rabone, Geoff 112, 114-115
Rait-Kerr, Diana 66
Ramadhin, Sonny 78
Ramphele, Mamphela 181
Reddick, Tom 13, 70
Reeve, Sir Anthony 162
Reid, ABJ 94
Reid, Frank 93
Reid, JA 94

Reid, John 55, 112, 171
Rhodes, Cecil v, 11, 16, 93
Rhodes, Wilfred 76
Richards, Barry 70, 168, 186
Richardson, Peter 123, 125, 130, 134
Rimmer, Gordon 41
Risien, Bruce 160, 166
Roberts, Vic 25, 49
Robertson-Glasgow, RC 41, 78
Robins, Derrick 158
Robinson, Basil 31
Robinson, Emmott 77
Rogers, Clive 149-150
Rood, Pearce 161, 166
Rothschild, Gerald 61, 75
Rowan, Athol 15, 75, 97, 99, 102-104, 107, 131
Rowan, Eric 16, 71, 96-97, 99, 101, 106, 108, 112
Roy, Hugh 117
Rudd, Robin 108, 125

S

Sauer, Paul 91
Saulnier, Serge 27-28
Schock, Philip 152-154, 161
Scott, CP 76
Sheppard, David 169-170
Sherwell, PW 54
Sibiya, Siya 95
Simpson, Bobby 135
Simpson, RT 58, 98, 101
Sisulu, Walter 179
Smith, JV 37
Smith, Mike 171
Smuts, General 138, 141
Snitcher, Harry 154
Sobers, Gary 78, 168
Sobukwe, Robert 179
Soro, Robert 41, 45

Stanford, Walter 141
Stanley, Major 25
Statham, Brian 123, 127, 129
Steele-Bodger, Micky 25, 50, 52
Steenkamp, Dr 140
Stevenson, MH 56
Stewart, Alan 23
Steyn, Judge Jan 95, 160
Steytler, Dr Jan 141, 179
Strydom, Dr 139
Sutcliffe, Bert 55, 112-115, 136, 171
Sutcliffe, Jim 165
Suzman, Dr Mosie 179
Suzman, Helen vi, 141, 147, 178-183
Swanton, Jim 74, 77-78
Swarbrick, David 27
Swart, Peter 71
Swart, Ray 141, 178
Swire, Sir John 61

T

Tanner, Haydn 25, 40-41, 51
Tanner, John 56
Tattersall, Roy 99-100
Taufel, Simon 186
Tayfield, Hugh 97, 102, 111, 114,
    116-117, 123, 126-131, 135-136
Taylor, Gill 160
Taylor, Herby 80, 94
Tebbutt, Judge Pat 160
Terblanche, Colonel 147
Thatcher, Margaret 174
Toshack, Ernie 34
Travers, Jika 31, 47
Trueman, Freddie 54, 170-171
Trypanis, Constantine 62
Tshwete, Steve 162
Tsolikele, Thami 161
Tutu, Archbishop Desmond 181
Tyson, Frank 78, 123, 128

V

van Beuge, Tex 160, 166
van Ryneveld, Mark 139, 140, 183
van Ryneveld, Tony 17, 24, 38, 59, 161
van Ryneveld, Verity vii, 12, 35-36,
    139, 175, 178, 183
van Ryneveld, Philip 139, 140, 175
van Ryneveld, Tessa (Kirkaldy) 139, 140
van Zyl Slabbert, Frederik 147
van Zyl Steyn, Johan 19
van der Bijl, Pieter 13
van der Bijl, Vincent 184
van der Merwe, Peter 94, 192
Varachia, Rashid 157
Verity, Hedley 100
Verwoerd, Dr HF 91, 139, 143, 147, 181
Viljoen, Ken 120, 135
Vintcent, CL 67
Vintcent, Nelles 37, 60
Vorster, John 156

W

Waddell, Herbert 50
Wade, Herbert 80
Waite, Johnny 97, 101, 106, 117,
    125-126, 132, 134, 136
Wakefield, Sir Wavell 108
Waldegrave, Lord 176
Wallace, Merv 55-56, 171
Walsh, Courtney 186
Wardle, Johnny 32, 54, 89, 99-100, 123,
    126-127, 129
Warner, Sir Pelham vi, 54, 66, 108
Warton, Major 86
Watson 32, 54, 103-104
Waugh, Steve 186
Webb, Hugh 35, 64
Wemyss, Jock 50
West, Stewart 91

Westcott, Dick 114, 117, 118
Weston, Garfield 152
Whitcombe, Philip 31, 35, 53-54, 56, 64
Wild, Rev John 19
Wild, Margaret 22
Wiley, Jim 92-93
Wiley, John 13
Williams, Bleddyn 25, 40-41, 50
Williams, Les 40
Williams, Owen Townley 141
Wilson, Gully 37, 47
Wilson, Trevor 23
Winn, Chris 54, 56
Woodcock, John iii, vi, vii, 79, 130
Woods, Donald 138
Wooller, Wilf 40
Woolmer, Bob 13, 160
Worsley, Kate 108
Worsley, Sir William 108, 109
Wrigley, Mike 56
Wyatt, Bob 171

Y

Yardley, Norman 54, 59, 108
Young, Martin 13

Z

Zille, Helen 182, 192